SAT®
READING

✔

ADVANCED

PRACTICE
SERIES

◇ For the Redesigned SAT

◇ Full Tests and Section Scores

◇ Essential Tips and Tactics

ies
TEST
PREP

Created by
Arianna Astuni, President IES
Khalid Khashoggi, CEO IES

Editorial
Patrick Kennedy, Executive Editor
Christopher Carbonell, Editorial Director
Rajvi Patel, Editor
Caitlin Hoynes-O'Connor, Editor
Yasmine Gharib, Assistant Editor

Design
Kay Kang, www.kaygraphic.com

Authors

Arianna Astuni	Caitlin Hoynes-O'Connor
Danielle Barkley	Nathaniel Hunt
Larry Bernstein	Charles Kennedy
Christopher Carbonell	Patrick Kennedy
Robert Collins	Khalid Khashoggi
Cynthia Helzner	Paul King
Nancy Hoffman	Rajvi Patel
Chris Holliday	Cassidy Yong

Published by IES Publications
www.IESpublications.com
© IES Publications, 2015

ON BEHALF OF
Integrated Educational Services, Inc.
355 Main Street
Metuchen, NJ 08840
www.ies2400.com

We would like to thank the IES Publications team as well as the teachers and students at IES2400 who have contributed to the creation of this book. We would also like to thank our Chief Marketing Officer, Sonia Choi, for her invaluable input.

The SAT® is a registered trademark of the College Board, which was not involved in the production of, and does not endorse, this product.

ISBN-10: 0-9964064-0-9
ISBN-13: 978-0-9964064-0-6

QUESTIONS OR COMMENTS? Visit us at ies2400.com

TABLE OF CONTENTS

Need an answer explained?
Visit ies2400.com/answers

To arrange group or private tutoring at one of our locations, please visit **ies2400.com** or e-mail us at **sat2400@ies2400.com**.

*Your personal information will be kept confidential and will never be sold to third parties. IES may contact you periodically with special offers, updated information and new services. Any e-mail sent by IES will provide the option to be removed from the e-mail mailing list.

Dear student,

Of all the sections on the SAT, Reading has always been among the most practice-intensive. I remember that my students taking the pre-2016, pre-redesign SAT would always request new critical reading passages and new vocabulary exercises. Strong work in these areas was the key to the many high and perfect scores that have been a prominent part of IES history. While much is changing on the New 2016 SAT, there is one thing that this test and its predecessor have very much in common: practice, once again, is still the best way and often the only way to succeed on the SAT Reading.

That is exactly why we at IES have brought you this book. SAT Reading is indeed challenging—historically, the section that is hardest to ace—and is certainly intimidating at first glance. At second glance, though, you will see that the New SAT follows a structure that can be mastered and presents questions that can be solved easily and naturally through high familiarity. We at IES have spent the past several months analyzing the question types and passage content that will appear on the New SAT; we have relied on only the most up-to-date College Board material, and have crafted a book that reflects the best of our fifteen years of instruction. If you have already worked through the College Board Blue Book, these ten new tests will match the content that you will see when your test day arrives.

Get ready to excel on the New SAT. As you will discover, practice really does make perfect on the test's new reading section—but only when that practice is guided by the highest levels of quality and expertise. Each passage in this book has been tried out by students just like you. Each test is designed to capture the test-writing tricks and passage-writing styles favored by the College Board. And each answer explanation on ies2400.com is crafted to quickly yet insightfully show you how to eliminate false answers and find effective evidence for your answer choices. Everything you need to control the New SAT Reading is right here.

I wish you all the best in your test-taking endeavors!

Sincerely,

Arianna Astuni,
President, IES

SAT
Reading
Essentials

The New Structure of the
SAT Reading Test

Overview

Early in 2014, test-takers were alerted to major changes to both the SAT and the PSAT. The new version of the PSAT had its debut in October of 2015, while the new version of the SAT was administered for the first time in March of 2016. Although the New SAT will still challenge readers to work effectively with context clues and small details, there have been significant alterations to the format and emphasis of the SAT Reading section.

Here is a look at some of the major changes:

> **✓ Remember**
>
> Despite changes in format, the SAT is still an evidence-based test. Other than relatively advanced vocabulary, you DO NOT need much specialized knowledge. Instead, you must focus on context clues and learn overarching strategies to succeed.

New SAT	Old SAT
The Reading score is combined with the Writing score for a single scaled score of 200-800.	The Reading score is given its own scaled score of 200-800; Writing is scored independently.
Four answer choices, no guessing penalty.	Five answer choices, 0.25 point guessing penalty.
Reading consists of five long reading comprehension passages.	Reading section consists of sentence completion problems, short passages, and long passages.
Topics occur in a set order, with an emphasis on social science, natural science, and prose fiction and no formal or consistent discussion of autobiography or the humanities.	Topics do not occur in a set order, and autobiography and the humanities may be treated on their own or may be discussed in passages that also treat social science and natural science topics.
Vocabulary is tested in Word in Context questions; readers are asked to determine the best, most relevant meaning of an advanced but not obscure word.	Vocabulary is tested in both Word in Context and Sentence Completion questions: highly obscure vocabulary may be used.
Graphics and visuals are included for analysis and linked to questions in Reading.	Graphics and visuals are used only in the Mathematics sections.
Command of Evidence questions require test-takers to find the best evidence for a previous answer.	No directly and explicitly linked questions, though multiple questions may refer to the same topic.

New SAT Essentials

Reading Test

Each Reading Test will follow exactly the same positioning and roughly the same structure. Reading is the very first section that test-takers will encounter on the New SAT, and will always adhere to the following content and timing standards:

65
MINUTES
to complete
Five Passages

52
QUESTIONS
at 10-11 Questions
per Passage

The different passages themselves will also break down in a manner that should be familiar to test-takers well in advance:

♦ FIVE Passages per test, each passage between 500 and 750 words. The total word count for all passages will be 3250 words

♦ FOUR Topic Areas, which always occur in the following order: 1) Fiction, 2) Social Science, 3) Natural Science (first), 4) Global Conversation, 5) Natural Science (second)

♦ ONE Paired Passage reading and TWO Passages with graphics. A Paired Passage may occur in any of the Topic Areas except for Fiction; a graphic may occur in any of the Topic Areas except for Fiction and Global Conversation.

The Four Topic Areas for the New SAT Reading

Fiction: excerpts from novels and short stories, published between the eighteenth century and the present. The New SAT has prioritized written works that feature discernible conflicts or objectives and only a few principal characters.

Social Science: short essays and excerpts on economics, urban studies, transportation and infrastructure, careers and occupations, ethics and morality. A reading in this area will typically have a strong thesis supported by data, case studies, observed trends, and other evidence.

Natural Science: articles and excerpts discussing experiments and data, often with an emphasis on new knowledge or changing theories, in biology, chemistry, ecology, physics, astronomy, psychology, and related topics

Global Conversation: thesis-oriented documents, speeches, and excerpts from major politicians and important historical figures. These readings can range in date from the eighteenth century to the present day.

Major Reading Question Types

Primary Purpose or Main Idea

These questions require you to give an accurate synopsis of the entire passage, often with a focus on the position or situation described.

Content and Characterization

You may be asked, for these questions, to identify what is explicitly stated or asserted by the author. You may also need to give a summary of the tone of a portion of the passage.

Word in Context

For these questions, you will need to consider four possible meanings of a single word or phrase and decide which meaning is logically appropriate to the context given by the passage.

Purpose, Function, and Developmental Pattern

These questions require attention to the fine points of device and structure, both for individual lines and for the passage as a whole.

Inference and Suggestion

Questions such as these require you to draw logical conclusions from passage content. Do NOT misread these as opportunities to interpret the passage or use outside knowledge.

Command of Evidence

Often linked to specific Content or Inference questions, Command of Evidence questions ask you to provide evidence for previous answers by choosing specific, justifying line references.

Graphics and Evidence

These questions may ask you to analyze a graphic (chart, table, map, diagram) on its own, or may ask you to compare the content of a graphic to the content of the passage it accompanies.

1

Which choice best summarizes the passage?

A) A young man accepts a job that proves to be unexpectedly rewarding.
B) A young man achieves new insights by making a dramatic lifestyle change.
C) A young man deals with the whims of an unfair employer.
D) A young man questions the value and utility of his university education.

2

Ms. Kurimoto addresses the narrator in a manner that can best be characterized as

A) bewildered.
B) cautious.
C) downcast.
D) amused.

3

As used in line 16, "deliver" most nearly means

A) provide.
B) fulfill.
C) rescue.
D) transport.

4

The main purpose of the fifth paragraph (lines 45-57) is to

A) summarize an argument that the author rejects.
B) offer statistical evidence for an unpopular view.
C) describe an experiment that is inherently flawed.
D) question the methods used in a recent study.

5

Based on information in the passage, it can reasonably be inferred that the Goblin Shark

A) has only recently been studied by ecologists.
B) inhabits ecosystems that are difficult to explore.
C) has altered its behavior in response to natural disasters.
D) is of greater interest to non-specialists than to trained biologists.

6

Which choice provides the best evidence for the answer to the previous question?

A) Lines 2-3 ("It was . . . statistics")
B) Lines 18-20 ("Despite such . . . Goblin Shark")
C) Lines 47-51 ("When Leary . . . Goblin Shark")
D) Lines 68-72 ("Ecologists . . . after all")

7

Do the data in the chart support the author's claims about "online merchandising" (lines 34-39)?

A) Yes, because the data show that such merchandising is unregulated.
B) Yes, because the data indicate a proliferation of small online merchants.
C) No, because the data only account for merchants based in the United States.
D) No, because the data indicate a decrease in merchandising revenues.

New SAT Essentials

Test-Taking Tips

In order to make sure that you are answering questions accurately and efficiently, keep in mind the following pieces of New SAT Reading advice:

◆ Know the amount of time that you will need to read through each passage for effective comprehension. As you read through, try to get a sense of the author's topic, tone, and possible thesis: there will often be questions on exactly these issues.

◆ DO NOT re-read portions of a passage, and DO NOT bog yourself down with note-taking. Many students are accustomed to taking notes for future consultation and use. On the SAT, notes of this sort and the thinking habits that go with them are both counter-productive.

◆ If you are switching from the Old SAT to the New SAT, be aware that the New SAT will often avoid giving specific line references in its questions. Instead, a detail or an idea from the passage may be cited, without the exact lines that the Old SAT so often provided. Use a strong initial read to get a sense of major details and passage structure.

◆ Word in Context questions require careful analysis. At times, the expected "dictionary definition" of a word will be incorrect; instead, a meaning that might not come to mind immediately will be the best answer. Always use clues from the passage, and always replace the word in the passage with your answer word to make sure that your choice is logical.

◆ Command of Evidence questions can be daunting at first, but can actually help you to work through a passage and its questions with great efficiency. For instance, if you are having trouble with the question IMMEDIATELY BEFORE a Command of Evidence question, look at the Command of Evidence line references and see if they put you on track to the best answer to the previous question.

Once you have become accustomed to methods such as these, be VERY CAUTIOUS of double-guessing. The ten tests in this book give you the opportunity to practice on the New SAT Reading until your test-taking instincts are sound. If you go against some of those well-developed instincts, you will be cheating yourself out of right answers.

NEXT STEPS: Now that you know exactly what to expect on the New SAT Reading, you will need consistent practice to become fully familiar with the test's material. Effective timing and excellent attention to detail are going to be your keys to success. If you need help, visit ies2400.com.

TEST 1

Test 1

Reading Test
65 MINUTES, 52 QUESTIONS

Turn to Section 1 of your answer sheet to answer the questions in this section.

DIRECTIONS

Each passage or pair of passages below is followed by a number of questions. After reading each passage or pair, choose the best answer to each question based on what is stated or implied in the passage or passages and in any accompanying graphics (such as a table or graph).

Questions 1-10 are based on the following passage.

This passage explores the narrator's development into a young adult through her relationship with her mother.

I clamber out of the bumble bee bus that chugs to a stop outside my house, run through the wide front door, and skid to a stop in the kitchen where my mother stands waiting. She turns
Line to me and follows the age-old tradition of asking how my first
5   day of school was. As I settle down for my afternoon snack, she begins to fill out all the school forms I've brought home—forms for emergency contact, lunch orders, PFA membership, photo censorship, medical allowances, forms for individual teachers, the works.
10   "Mom?" I ask, wiping my chin clean of juice, "what's that blue paper for?"
    She doesn't look up from her pen but replies in Chinese, "It's asking what allergies you have."
    "I don't have any, right?"
15   "Right," she says and swiftly checks off a few more boxes before planting her sweeping signature on the bottom of the page.
    "And this one?" I ask, peering over her shoulder. "It says . . . 'siblings . . . age . . . school . . .' Are they asking about sis?"
20   "Mhm."
    "She's in fourth grade, right? I can't wait until I'm that old!"
    "And then you can fill out these forms by yourself," she replies, switching to English, and gives me a smile.
25   I still remember that day, and the many more like it, when my mother gave me a look that made me wonder when I would grow up. At the time, growing up seemed like an impossibility. The future was a dip in a road obscured by mist, while my mother was a more tangible presence that
30   stood next to me. It's weird, though, how soon you reach the dip and how quickly the mist disappears to reveal a new path.
    I push open the front door and walk into the kitchen where my mother sits in front of her computer, her brows arched in frustration. I'm a high school student now and, with routine
35   casualness, I sling my backpack onto an empty chair and walk over to my mother.
    "Back from school? Anyway, can you help me with this? I just can't understand what they're asking me."
    Without a word, I commandeer my mother's computer
40   and peruse her screen; she is inspecting an online questionnaire from a hotel we've stayed at recently. "They're just asking us how our stay was, mom, things like room service quality."
    "Oh well, can you fill it out for me?"
45   "But it's so simple, mom, they're just asking—"
    "No no, I know, but you can fill it out for me."
    The next day she asks me to proofread an e-mail to a friend because her English grammar, in her opinion, is quite deficient. The day after that, I am called to look over her resume
50   so that she can find another job. A week later, I help her answer questions at the customs office while we get our passports approved. When I get the annual deluge of forms from school, my pen marks its way through all of them, leaving only the line at the bottom of each page for a parent's signature. And one day,
55   I muse, I'll be helping her sign that for me too.
    It's a Chinese tradition, though, that when children grow up they must take care of their parents. It's a responsibility that grows with the children; when you are very young, you are allowed to be innocent and ignorant because you do not
60   understand, but when you grow up and your mind widens, you must accept a series of new revelations and responsibilities. My mother's brief moments of helplessness occasionally remind me of myself when I was still in grade school, but maybe they're

CONTINUE

actually signs that she is growing even older. It's a thought
65 that I can't quite wrap my mind around yet, but I know that
while she grows, I grow too. That's why, when she asks me
for help, I habitually take a deep breath and reply in English,
"Sure, I can fill out those forms for you."

1

This passage can best be described as

A) a stirring recollection of a parent who is no longer part
of the narrator's life.

B) an account of the psychological pressures facing
Asian-American students.

C) a rumination on the nature of a particular family
responsibility.

D) a discussion of the dangers that individual desires pose
to traditional family structures.

2

When the narrator initially brings home school-related
papers (lines 1-24), she is

A) curious about the purposes served by the forms.

B) oblivious to the stress the forms bring her mother.

C) intrusive in demanding that her mother read the forms
for her.

D) puzzled that her mother does not know sufficient
English to fill out the forms.

3

As used in line 16, "planting" most nearly means

A) seeding.

B) placing.

C) settling.

D) cultivating.

4

The mother's remark about fourth grade in line 23 ("And
then . . . yourself") can best be described as

A) foreshadowing.

B) threatening.

C) apologetic.

D) admonishing.

5

The "dip" discussed in lines 28 and 31 expresses the
author's sense that growing up

A) is a descent into an unpleasant world of responsibilities
and hardship.

B) seems too distant to be real until one actually grows up.

C) can change one's life instantly and irrevocably.

D) requires a period of confusion followed by steady
advancement.

6

It can be inferred from the passage that the narrator's role in
helping her mother fill out forms is

A) a purely sentimental means of expressing her love for her
mother.

B) a service which may become requested even more often
as time passes.

C) an irritating intervention in her mother's affairs.

D) a clever way of avoiding more pressing obligations
within her family.

7

Which choice provides the best evidence for the answer to
the previous question?

A) Lines 25-28 ("I still . . . impossibility")

B) Lines 47-49 ("The next . . . deficient")

C) Lines 52-55 ("When I . . . too")

D) Lines 66-68 ("That's why . . . you")

8

As used in line 52, "deluge" most nearly means

A) wealth.

B) load.

C) attack.

D) calamity.

9

The narrator views her duties to her mother as

A) an unfair burden that she wishes to relinquish.

B) an affectionate gesture motivated by the unique relationship she shares with her mother.

C) an occasion for reflection on the nature of maturity.

D) an unnecessary but well-known custom that she maintains out of nostalgia.

10

Which choice provides the best evidence for the answer to the previous question?

A) Lines 5-9 ("As I settle . . . works")

B) Lines 44-46 ("Oh well . . . me")

C) Lines 56-57 ("It's a Chinese . . . their parents")

D) Lines 61-64 (My mother's . . . older")

Questions 11-21 are based on the following passage and supplementary material.

The following passage was written by a historian who studies how governments address issues in ecology. Here, the author considers the role of nature, particularly state-owned forests, in French society.

While many people are aware that France is a country of rivers—the Seine, the Loire, the Rhone, the Garonne—few people are aware that France is also a country of woods and
Line forests. Surprisingly, ten percent of all the forests in Europe are
5 to be found in France. Unsurprisingly, the French are deeply attached to these stretches of nature, and with good reason. Since 1556, by a law that cannot be changed, the *forêts dominiales*[1] have belonged to the people of France for their needs and use. The English may cherish rural walks among the green
10 woodlands of their country, but for the most part their ancient woodlands have been urbanized (as in the case of the New Forest in Hampshire, where the smells and scents of the countryside have been smothered by the stink of petrol and diesel fumes) or industrialized by the Forestry Commission (as in
15 Northumberland, where serried ranks of fir cover the landscape in blank anonymity). The real, ancient forest that once covered England has been dissipated and degraded. This is not so in France: the forests are not regarded as expendable. This is not to say that they have remained untouched for the last five hundred
20 years. The need for direct communication between towns and cities has meant that roads and high speed rail lines have been permitted, but these have not been allowed to impose on the land, which is why transit routes are so direct and straight, with the occasional *aires*[2] where motorists may pause, sit at wooden
25 tables and benches, and wander a little into the untarnished woods, before continuing the journey to the next town and experiencing once again the staccato pace of modern life.
They are calm, these woods with their glades of wildflowers and ferns and their occasional swaths of heathland: calm, but not
30 without activity. Clouds of butterflies celebrate among the shafts of sunlight that pierce through the leafy branches of sturdy oak, smooth beech, and silver birch. Birds, of course, nest and flit and hunt; at dusk, owls sail past, silent and deadly. Rabbit and hare, fox and badger are here. Sit for a while on the gnarled roots of an
35 ancient oak, and you will soon become aware of the presence of deer. Perhaps, if you are very still, you will be privileged to see a stag stepping regally and silently through a nearby clearing. I doubt that you will have the luck to see wild boar, but they are here, in the inner reaches of the forest.
40 There is a human presence, of course. These forests are not abandoned, but are tended by foresters. Trees are felled to provide the logs for wood stoves, still a major form of heating in the towns and villages of rural France. One cubic meter of logs for a stove will last a week, and a forester can often sell you this

CONTINUE ➡

45 quantity for about 50 euros. The foresters are the gardeners of this ancient woodland, coppicing it and replanting it, ensuring its survival; they are also responsible for the culling and pruning necessary to keep the woods alive. Between September and March, hunting is permitted—if you have the correct permission
50 forms, that is. French hunting is not like English hunting: the French relish the pursuit, but not necessarily the killing, of animals. Hounds are used for scenting, not slaughter. The huntsmen here often seem more relaxed than their English counterparts, and the curled French hunting horn produces a
55 sound much more tuneful than the English bray. French hunting is not a contest between man and animal: it is much more of a social event on horseback. Of course, if you want to join in the hunt, you have to belong to an established group and must complete mountains of paperwork, in a uniquely French
60 bureaucratic fashion.

   Regardless, at any time, without asking anyone's permission, any citizen may enter a French forest and pick the wild fruits and berries and mushrooms. Any citizen can walk through the forest at any time, alone or with family, with a dog,
65 with whomever. These forests belong to every citizen, as they have for centuries. They are the national heritage or, as it is called in French, *le patrimoine*.[3]

1 *forêts dominiale*s: forests owned by the state
2 *aires*: rest stops
3 *le patrimoine*: national heritage

11

The primary purpose of the passage is to

A) consider the value of forests in French contemporary culture.
B) denounce the urbanization of forests in England.
C) briefly explain the differences between French and English wildlife.
D) examine the role of humans in the destruction of European forests.

12

The author uses the images in the second paragraph to

A) suggest that the French forests are full of wildlife.
B) enumerate a few of the animal species that are unique to the French woods.
C) encourage the reader to visit the forests.
D) stress the importance of caution and stillness when observing wild animals.

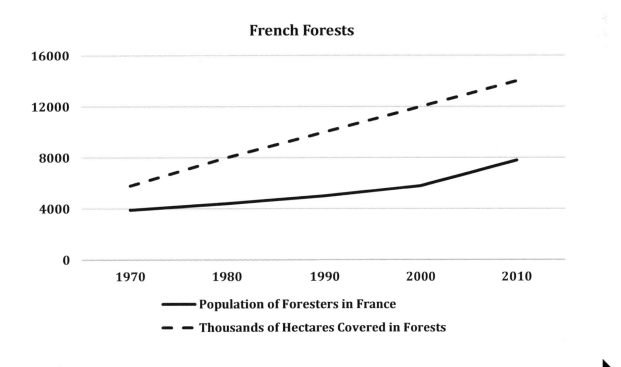

French Forests

— Population of Foresters in France
- - Thousands of Hectares Covered in Forests

13

The author draws comparisons between France and England primarily in order to

A) indicate that the French and the English tend to their forests in surprisingly similar ways.

B) claim that the French have a greater appreciation for wildlife.

C) show that England has more undeveloped land than France does.

D) deny that the English and the French have any important political or cultural values in common.

14

Which choice provides the best evidence for the answer to the previous question?

A) Lines 4-5 ("Surprisingly . . . France")

B) Lines 37-39 ("I doubt . . . forest")

C) Lines 48-50 ("Between . . . that is")

D) Lines 50-52 ("French . . . animals")

15

According to the passage, the French attitude towards the human development of forests is best described as one of

A) disdain.

B) pragmatism.

C) ambivalence.

D) enthusiasm.

16

Which choice provides the best evidence for the answer to the previous question?

A) Lines 9-11 ("The English . . . urbanized")

B) Lines 20-23 ("The need . . . the land")

C) Lines 61-63 ("Regardless . . . mushrooms")

D) Lines 66-67 ("They . . . *le patrimoine*")

17

According to the passage, the forests belong to the French citizens because of

A) an ideological revolution.

B) a permanent law.

C) a recent innovation.

D) a popular custom.

18

As used line 42, "form" most nearly means

A) structure.

B) measure.

C) shape.

D) method.

19

As used in line 59, "mountains" most nearly means

A) ranges.

B) hills.

C) piles.

D) supplies.

20

According to the graph, the number of hectares covered by forests in France has

A) only increased by a trivial measure.

B) grown exponentially.

C) decreased by 50%.

D) increased steadily since 1970.

21

Which of the following is implicitly stated in the graph and explicitly stated in the passage?

A) Logging and hunting have had a detrimental effect on the diversity of trees in France.

B) The increase of land covered with forests is largely due to increased conservation efforts by the French government.

C) Foresters are largely responsible for cultivating, maintaining, and preserving the woodlands.

D) The increased population of foresters was initially beneficial but has caused more damage in recent years.

Test 1

Questions 22-31 are based on the following passages.

The following two passages discuss the phenomenon of computer-generated literature. The first passage is taken from a 2003 news column on new media and innovation, while the second is from a 2006 article on successful story-creating computer systems.

Passage 1

"A seven eve will typify the gaudy scoop. A typed euros will gaily gauche the scaly scampi. The twiggy jived hence erupts the viable vision."

Line 5 Believe it or not, those three sentences were taken from a book. It's a virtual book, a digital product of The Literature Factory, which is a computer program that acts as a kind of automated "writer" that compiles letters into words, words into sentences, and sentences into a book-length work.

Andy Fundinger made The Literature Factory for use in
10 Second Life, a three-dimensional online environment where multiple users can build digital objects and interact with one another. An engineer by training, Fundinger took an interest in the project that was technical rather than literary. Nonetheless, his inspiration came from a well-loved book, *One Two Three*
15 *Infinity* by physicist George Gamow. In this classic text, which explores the possible applications of math and science, Gamow describes a long automatic printing press that prints books on its own, thus circumventing the need for human authors altogether.

20 Fundinger thought that scripting an approximation of this idea into Second Life would be an interesting challenge, so he went to work, using a couple of his own desktop computers as external servers. Two other programmers designed visuals for the "factory." Virtual visitors can look down from grated
25 walkways and watch as large cylinders called Word-o-Mats spin through different letter combinations, discarding nonsensical ones until they make proper English words. The words are then picked up by smiling robots that drop them one by one into different bins.

30 The behind-the-scenes functionality is relatively simple. The Word-o-Mats make a request to the server, which checks the letter combinations against a dictionary to make sure that the word is real. That word is then sent back to Second Life and into a bin, which checks periodically with the server to find out
35 when new words have been created. Meanwhile, the sentence-maker connects to the server every 90 seconds and tells it to make a sentence from the words in the bin using one of a few basic sentence forms, such as noun-verb-the-adjective-noun. As the sentences are created, they are copied into a digital book,
40 thus creating a work of literature—or something like it.

Passage 2

With his artificial intelligence-based computer system MEXICA, Rafael Pérez y Pérez is exploring the place where creativity and automation meet. Fed only basic details, MEXICA is able to generate very short stories, mini-epics
45 about love and violence between knights, kings, and other ancient inhabitants of México City—people known as the Mexicas.

Though the stories are short and simple in construction, readers gave them high marks for coherence, structure, content,
50 and feeling of suspense. In an online survey that asked readers to compare stories produced by MEXICA, other computer systems, and one written entirely by a person, a story created by MEXICA was ranked the highest.

Computerized storytellers similar to MEXICA have been
55 in existence since the 1970s. So what is it that makes this system uniquely successful? In a paper introducing MEXICA, Pérez y Pérez, a researcher at Autonomous Metropolitan University in México City, writes that although emotions are an integral part of the creative process, many
60 computer models of creativity do not account for them. MEXICA, on the other hand, attempts to do this by tagging characters with their emotional connection to each other, then using those connections to drive plot development. To some extent, it functions like the creative writer who says she
65 "knows" her characters but not exactly what the characters will do or how the story will end until she begins writing.

Machine-made art can be unnerving, yet the value of MEXICA lies not in replacing human creators but in teaching us how the creative process works. For example, in designing
70 a building, an architect relies on blueprints and scale models, which are tools that help him to externalize and better understand his own ideas. Likewise, computers are tools that can help people to visualize complex systems. We are far from being able to create a system capable of making literature like
75 human beings do, but if we can build a system that generates adequate short stories, we can gain a better understanding of how literature is created.

22

As used in line 18, "circumventing" most nearly means
A) being cautious of.
B) exhibiting tact about.
C) avoiding.
D) evading.

23

As used in line 60, "account for" most nearly means

A) consider.

B) analyze.

C) record.

D) constitute.

24

It can most reasonably be inferred that the computer system described in Passage 2 differs from that described in Passage 1 primarily because it

A) uses an automated process to create short stories.

B) integrates emotions into short stories.

C) is designed for use on the Internet.

D) generates stories about Mexican history.

25

Which choice provides the best evidence for the answer to the previous question?

A) Lines 41-43 ("With . . . meet")

B) Lines 48-50 ("Though . . . suspense")

C) Lines 54-55 ("Computerized . . . 1970s")

D) Lines 61-63 ("MEXICA . . . development")

26

According to Passage 1, Andy Fundinger was motivated to create The Literature Factory because he

A) gravitated to the engineering aspects of the project.

B) wanted to publish ground-breaking research.

C) sensed the possibility of making a profit.

D) desired to contribute to contemporary literature.

27

Which choice provides the best evidence for the answer to the previous question?

A) Lines 4-5 ("Believe . . . book")

B) Lines 12-13 ("An engineer . . . literary")

C) Lines 27-29 ("The words . . . bins")

D) Lines 30-33 ("The behind-the-scenes . . . real")

28

The author of Passage 1 uses the phrase "or something like it" in line 40 to imply that the stories produced by The Literature Factory are

A) similar to other works.

B) grammatically incorrect.

C) easy to interpret.

D) basically nonsense.

29

The author of Passage 2 would most likely reply to George Gamow's ideas by saying that

A) machines cannot satisfactorily replace human writers.

B) mechanized writing has existed since the late 1900s.

C) printing presses will never become fully automatic.

D) computers can only write short, simple stories.

30

The primary purpose of the last paragraph of Passage 2 is to suggest that

A) intelligence-simulating computer systems can help us to understand creativity.

B) there are several parallels between literature and architectural design.

C) computers can be used to produce blueprints and scale models.

D) emotions are an important aspect of literature.

31

According to Passage 2, it can most reasonably be inferred that the stories created by MEXICA are

A) inferior to those created by The Literature Factory.

B) not disjointed or predictable.

C) lacking in emotional content.

D) inspired by a well-known book.

CONTINUE

Test 1

Questions 32-41 are based on the following passage.

The following is an excerpt from *The Old World and Its Ways*, a travel narrative published by American activist and politician William Jennings Bryan in 1907.

One who travels in foreign lands is likely to learn but little of the governments of the lands through which he passes, unless he makes a special effort to inform himself, for the
Line lines of travel are laid through the communities where law and
5 order are maintained and where the government is so stable that the casual observer has no occasion to investigate its inner workings. The mountains tower above him, and he sees them; the chasms yawn before him and he beholds them; and the various forms of agriculture leave a panoramic effect upon his
10 memory. He frequently meets the merchant in his store, sees the laborer at his work quite often, and occasionally beholds a grandee in his carriage; but not being able to speak the language of the country he learns little about the forms of government and less about the political aspirations of the people; and yet the
15 science of government is one of the most important sciences, and the "royal art," as it has been called, stands first among the arts. Tolstoy has declared that the science which teaches us how to live is the most important of sciences, and surely the science of government comes next. While it is true that an individual
20 can by misbehavior forfeit the blessings of good government, or by good behavior minimize the evils of bad government—while it is true that no government, however good, can save a man from himself if he is determined to throw himself away, and that no government, however bad, can entirely deprive
25 him of the rewards of virtue, yet governments may do much to encourage or to hinder the development of the people.
　　Governments may retard or advance the material growth of a country. For instance, our government is in part, at least, responsible for the unparalleled development of the United
30 States, because it has given the largest encouragement to the individual. The Japanese government has in like manner stimulated education by the establishment of a public school system and has developed a large number of public men by the organization of a parliamentary system. Turkey, on the other
35 hand, has blighted some of the fairest portions of the earth by suppressing political independence, by ignoring education, and by leaving the industrious citizen at the mercy of the marauder. There has been little political life in Turkey because few of the people have had the education necessary to take a broad
40 survey of the country and its needs, while great stretches of fertile country lie uncultivated because the government is so indifferent to the rights of the people that the tiller of the soil has no assurance that he will be allowed to harvest the crop which he plants. Those who have investigated the subject
45 contend that the valley of the Jordan would be a fruitful region if protection were given to those who would cultivate it, but

because the Bedouin has been allowed to come down from the hillside and reap where he has not sown, the land is neglected.

32

Which of the following best describes the developmental pattern of the passage?

A) An explanation of some of the practical obstacles facing travelers, followed by descriptions of countries where those obstacles may be easily avoided

B) An endorsement of a political theory, followed by an assessment of how different cultures have reacted to this theory

C) A critique of the limited perspective of a particular group, followed by a series of recommendations for broadening this group's perspective

D) A discussion of the difficulties involved in a particular line of inquiry, followed by examples illustrating a single point

33

In the first paragraph, Bryan characterizes travelers in foreign lands as

A) most strongly affected by natural landscapes.

B) easily deceived by the propaganda of local authorities.

C) intrigued by questions of government but lacking academic training.

D) uninformed about important aspects of their surroundings.

34

Which choice provides the best evidence for the answer to the previous question?

A) Lines 7-8 ("The mountains . . . beholds them")

B) Lines 10-12 ("He frequently . . . carriage")

C) Lines 12-14 ("but not being . . . the people")

D) Lines 14-17 ("the science . . . the arts")

35

As used in line 26, "encourage" most nearly means

A) praise.

B) cultivate.

C) persuade.

D) influence.

CONTINUE

36

A main premise of Bryan's views of government is that

A) an effective government creates opportunities for political participation.

B) democratic principles originating in the United States are rapidly being adopted elsewhere.

C) international travel creates the illusion that all governments are equally effective.

D) governments should assume few powers beyond the protection of private property.

37

The "assurance" in line 43 is best understood to refer to

A) the ability to earn a proper education in agricultural methods.

B) the guarantee that crops will not be seized by the Turkish government.

C) the certitude that property will be protected from Bedouin raiders.

D) the right to publicly criticize government policies without fear of retaliation.

38

It can be inferred that William Jennings Bryan views the role of government in daily life as

A) a subject that has been unfairly neglected by moralists.

B) a powerful influence that can have widely differing effects in different countries.

C) the primary factor that explains Japan's economic prosperity.

D) a possible explanation of why countries such as Turkey become liable to revolutionary regime change.

39

Which choice provides the best evidence for the answer to the previous question?

A) Lines 17-19 ("Tolstoy has . . . come next")

B) Lines 27-28 ("Governments . . . a country")

C) Lines 31-34 ("The Japanese . . . system")

D) Lines 34-37 ("Turkey . . . marauder")

40

As used in lines 39-40, "take a broad survey of" most nearly means

A) understand in a thorough manner.

B) describe in an impressionistic way.

C) provide a tentative estimate of.

D) journey in order to appreciate.

41

The "good government" and "bad government" described in the first paragraph are similar in that each

A) is meant to be understood as a purely theoretical construct.

B) is incapable of fully dictating individual behavior.

C) is unlikely to intervene in commerce and education.

D) is based on a system of unambiguous rewards and punishments.

CONTINUE

Questions 42-52 are based on the following passage and supplementary material.

Adapted from a recent essay by an astrophysicist, this passage describes how astronomers ascertain the existence of planets in faraway star systems.

Recently, astronomers have determined that two leading candidates on the list of potentially habitable planets do not, in fact, exist. Once thought to be orbiting Gliese 581, a red dwarf
Line star about 20 light years from Earth, Gliese 581d and 581g
5 seemed to satisfy all the major criteria of habitable planets: rocky surfaces, ambient temperatures that support liquid water, and masses similar to Earth's. These qualities led Stephen Vogt, head of the team of astronomers that discovered the planets in 2010, to declare that "the chances of life on these planets are
10 100 percent."

Several follow-up studies failed to find evidence of the existence of Gliese 581d and 581g. This was enough to raise doubts, but a recent study published in the journal *Science* has conclusively demonstrated that the original dataset was
15 misconstrued, thus eliminating any evidence of the two planets. In four years, these planets have gone from guaranteed harbors of life to stretches of empty space.

How does one mistake empty space for a planet? At a distance of 20 light years, visual confirmation of planetary
20 masses is not feasible. Extrasolar planets are therefore detected indirectly. In the case of the planets of the Gliese system, astronomers inferred the existence of planets by measuring changes in the Gliese star's radial velocity. The gravitational pull exerted by a planet on a star has a negligible, but measurable,
25 effect on the latter's location. As the planet orbits the star and the direction of gravity's pull shifts, the star exhibits a measurable wobble. This wobble creates a Doppler effect, causing the light emitted from the star to shift toward the red or blue end of the spectrum, depending on which side the planet is
30 on. Astronomers measure this shift, and from that can determine the location and size of the body that causes it.

For stellar systems with only one planet, statistics such as these are easy enough to calculate. The wobble becomes much more complicated for systems like Gliese 581, which has at
35 least 3 planets in orbit. To determine the location of one body, astronomers must mathematically cancel out the shifts caused by other known bodies. Vogt's team performed the necessary calculations, and the result suggested a planet in the Gliese system's habitable zone with an orbital period of 66 days. The
40 authors of the most recent study observed that Gliese 581 rotates roughly every 130 days, almost exactly double Gliese 581d's period. This tidy coincidence led them to suspect that Vogt's data could just as easily be explained by irregular stellar activity rotating on the surface of the star, which would cause a Doppler
45 shift in the same way and at the same time as the "wobble" caused by a planet. Stellar activity is much easier to detect than a planet's presence, and indeed the authors confirmed that such

activity on the surface of Gliese 581 correlated strongly with the 66-day pattern taken as 581d's period. Once this activity
50 was subtracted from the best calculations of Gliese 581's wobble, the signal interpreted as 581g—the best candidate for a life-supporting planet in the system—also vanished, while those of planets d, c, and e became stronger. Unfortunately, these planets are unlikely to be able to support life.
55 With that, two entries on the short list of potentially habitable extrasolar planets were unceremoniously crossed off. This mistake will constitute a disappointment for those who are invested in this search; for many, this mistake also undermines faith in the ability of science to ascertain the
60 truth about objects at enormous distances from Earth. Yet the methodological refinement necessary to reveal the mistake is characteristic of the advancement of scientific knowledge, which means that the Gliese "mishap" can be seen as a step forward. As science journalist Xaq Rzetelny put it, the new
65 observations of stellar activity on Gliese 581 may "play a large role in the discovery of future exoplanets, so understanding when and why it happens is an important step in the search for exoplanets bearing life."

42

The primary purpose of the first paragraph is to

A) criticize the quality of studies published in the journal *Science*.
B) introduce a theory disproved after further study.
C) suggest that Stephen Vogt should not be investigating habitable planets.
D) demonstrate the author's knowledge of astronomy.

43

According to the author, Gliese 581 is difficult to study because

A) it is 20 light years from Earth.
B) its existence is disputed by astronomers.
C) its study requires especially challenging mathematics.
D) its wobble involves multiple planets.

44

As used in line 16, "guaranteed' most nearly means

A) confident.
B) contracted.
C) promised.
D) definite.

CONTINUE

23

Visual Confirmation of Planetary Masses Based on Distance

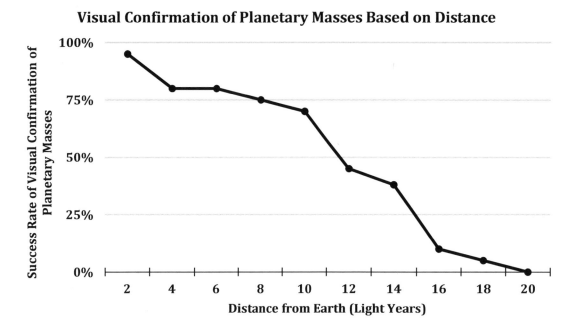

45

The question in line 18 ("How . . . planet?") serves to

A) suggest that the mistake was preposterous.

B) decry the carelessness of modern astronomers.

C) introduce the difficulty of detecting extrasolar planets.

D) imply that the existence of distant planets is impossible to prove.

46

It can most reasonably be inferred that Stephen Vogt's theory was

A) an intentional misrepresentation of evidence.

B) an undeniable proof of extraterrestrial life.

C) an accurate representation of Gliese 581.

D) a reasonable assumption based on data.

47

Which choice provides the best evidence for the answer to the previous question?

A) Lines 1-3 ("Recently . . . exist")

B) Lines 11-12 ("Several . . . 581g")

C) Lines 37-39 ("Vogt's team . . . days")

D) Lines 55-57 ("With that . . . off")   \

48

According to the author, Gliese 581 is significant because it

A) has orbiting planets capable of supporting life.

B) could contribute to the future study of life in space.

C) demonstrates the Doppler effect.

D) is a rare example of a red dwarf star.

49

Which choice provides the best evidence for the answer to the previous question?

A) Lines 3-5 ("Once thought . . . planets")

B) Lines 30-31 ("Astronomers . . . it")

C) Lines 39-42 ("The authors . . . period")

D) Lines 64-68 ("As science . . . life")

CONTINUE

50

As used in line 58, "invested in" most nearly means

A) supported by.

B) honored with.

C) committed to.

D) financed by.

51

Which of the following statements is best supported by the data in the graph?

A) Lines 7-10 ("These . . . percent")

B) Lines 12-15 ("This was . . . planets")

C) Lines 18-20 ("At a distance . . . feasible")

D) Lines 32-33 ("For stellar . . . calculate")

52

Do the data in the graph support the passage's discussion of the Doppler effect?

A) Yes, because as the distance increases from the Earth, the gravitational pull increases as well.

B) Yes, because the size and mass of a planet are directly proportional to radial velocity.

C) No, because extrasolar planetary masses can be detected through direct methods.

D) No, because the data in the graph are not explicitly linked to radial velocity.

STOP

If you finish before time is called, you may check your work on this section only.

Do not turn to any other section.

Answer Key: TEST 1

PASSAGE 1
Fiction

1. C
2. A
3. B
4. A
5. B
6. B
7. C
8. B
9. C
10. D

PASSAGE 2
Social Science

11. A
12. A
13. B
14. D
15. B
16. B
17. B
18. D
19. C
20. D
21. C

PASSAGE 3
Natural Science 1

22. C
23. A
24. B
25. D
26. A
27. B
28. D
29. A
30. A
31. B

PASSAGE 4
Global Conversation

32. D
33. D
34. C
35. B
36. A
37. C
38. B
39. B
40. A
41. B

PASSAGE 5
Natural Science 2

42. B
43. D
44. D
45. C
46. D
47. C
48. B
49. D
50. C
51. C
52. D

Once you have determined how many questions
you answered correctly, consult the chart on Page 174
to determine your **SAT Reading Test score.**

Please visit **ies2400.com/answers** for answer explanations.

Post-Test Analysis

This post-test analysis is essential if you want to see an improvement on your next test. Possible reasons for errors on the five passages in this test are listed here. Place check marks next to the types of errors that pertain to you, or write your own types of errors in the blank spaces.

TIMING AND ACCURACY

◇ Spent too long reading individual passages
◇ Spent too long answering each question
◇ Spent too long on a few difficult questions
◇ Felt rushed and made silly mistakes or random errors
◇ Unable to work quickly using textual evidence and POE
Other: _____

APPROACHING THE PASSAGES AND QUESTIONS

◇ Unable to effectively grasp a passage's tone or style
◇ Unable to effectively grasp a passage's topic or stance
◇ Did not understand the context of line references
◇ Did not eliminate false answers using strong evidence
◇ Answered questions using first impressions instead of POE
◇ Answered questions without checking or inserting final answer
◇ Eliminated correct answer during POE
◇ Consistent trouble with Word in Context vocabulary
◇ Consistent trouble with Command of Evidence questions
◇ Consistent trouble with passage comparison questions
Other: _____

> **Use this form** to better analyze your performance. If you don't understand why you made errors, there is no way that you can correct them!

FICTION: # CORRECT_____ # WRONG _____ # OMITTED _____

◇ Could not grasp the roles and attitudes of major characters
◇ Could not grasp the significance of particular scenes or images
◇ Difficulty understanding the author's style and language
◇ Difficulty understanding the tone, theme, and structure of the passage as a whole
Other: _____

SOCIAL SCIENCE AND
GLOBAL CONVERSATION: # CORRECT_____ # WRONG _____ # OMITTED _____

◇ Unable to grasp the overall argument or thesis of an individual passage
◇ Unable to work effectively with the specific data or evidence in a passage
◇ Unable to respond effectively to tone, structure, and vocabulary
◇ Difficulty working with the graphics and graphic questions in a Social Science passage
◇ Difficulty understanding the logic or methodology of a Social Science passage
◇ Difficulty with the style and language of a Global Conversation passage
◇ Difficulty with the main historical and political concepts of a Global Conversation passage
Other: _____

NATURAL SCIENCE: # CORRECT_____ # WRONG _____ # OMITTED _____

◇ Unable to grasp the overall argument or thesis of an individual passage
◇ Unable to work effectively with the specific data or evidence in a passage
◇ Unable to respond effectively to tone, structure, and vocabulary
◇ Difficulty understanding the significance of the theories or experiments presented
◇ Difficulty working with the graphics and graphic questions
Other: _____

TEST 2

Test 2

Reading Test
65 MINUTES, 52 QUESTIONS

Turn to Section 1 of your answer sheet to answer the questions in this section.

DIRECTIONS

Each passage or pair of passages below is followed by a number of questions. After reading each passage or pair, choose the best answer to each question based on what is stated or implied in the passage or passages and in any accompanying graphics (such as a table or graph).

Questions 1-10 are based on the following passage.

This passage is adapted from a work of contemporary fiction. In the episode that follows, Ms. Maitland is the headmistress at a respected boarding school.

Ms. Maitland's jaw was set tight. Her fingers tapped the desk irritably. Her mood had not been leavened at all by her arrival at the school. The caretaker had greeted her with the
Line news that the central heating was on the blink and would have
5 to be turned off for the morning, if not for the whole day. These tidings were followed by messages from three staff members, who were all suffering from the flu and were therefore absent. Ms. Maitland would have to delegate other instructors to cover their classes.
10 Ms. Maitland gritted her teeth and turned to the mail on her desk. The first letter was from a parent who hoped it would be alright to take her daughter for a week's holiday in Mallorca, since this was the only time of the year when they could get a cheap flight. This parent felt sure that her daughter would be
15 able to compensate for any important material that might be missed. (The girl was in the bottom set for her year, and very near the bottom of that.) "In any case," the mother had written, "I will keep an eye on her to make sure she completes all her schoolwork." Ms. Maitland gave a sardonic laugh and
20 wondered what the mother would be keeping her other eye on.
She pushed the button of her intercom.
"Janet?" She heard a gasp and a sound of hurried scuffling and whispering. "Janet, could you come in? And since I can hear that he is with you, please bring Mr. Boyce with you, if
25 you are both able to spare the time."
Ms. Maitland's lips compressed into a thin grim line; she snapped off the intercom, switched on the coffee maker, and began to take notes. She heard the door open. She completed

her notes and then looked up. Janet, her secretary, stood before
30 her, and positioned beside Janet—a deliberate space between them—was Tim Boyce, grinning with the vitality of carefree youth. He was dressed in sneakers, jeans, a T-shirt printed in lurid colors, and a leather jacket.
Ms. Maitland glared at Tim, and began to deliver her first
35 orders. "Mr. Boyce, it seems that Year 10 is without an art teacher this morning. Please supervise the class. I am informed that they are to continue with their fashion designs for the modern teenager. I have no doubt that you will be able to give some advice on this particular topic. The bell for class is about to
40 ring, so if you could arrive at the Art Studio before they run riot and absolutely demolish it, I would be grateful."
Tim raised his head as if to protest, but Ms. Maitland's expression was adamant. He shrugged his shoulders, then gave her a beaming smile. "Sure thing, Ms. Maitland. I'll jog all the
45 way. Have a nice day!" He turned and strode to the door, but then turned his head towards Janet. "Catch you later, Jan." Then he was gone.
Ms. Maitland allowed herself a sigh. "He cannot last," she thought. She turned to Janet and thawed a little. "We have a
50 great deal to get through this morning. Sit down, please, and take notes."
Janet said nothing. She pulled a chair to the desk and produced her notepad and pen. Ms. Maitland delivered her instructions in a precise, concise manner. Five minutes later, she
55 paused. She noted the dark circles beneath Janet's eyes.
"There's time for a coffee before we start, I think. I made a fresh pot. You are looking a little fatigued." Ms. Maitland gave a casual laugh. "I shouldn't be surprised to discover that you skipped breakfast this morning."
60 For a moment, Janet looked directly at Ms. Maitland. Then she grinned. "Out on the town last night. Not the best idea, in retrospect. It won't happen again."

Ms. Maitland's look was quizzical. "Do you mean that it won't happen again this week?" she asked "Or ever, or just
65 with Tim?" Janet was about to respond, but Ms. Maitland continued. "Oh yes, I know: you are grown up now and living your own life, but I do worry sometimes about you, you know. It is only natural to care about one's employees."
Janet sighed and smiled. "Yes, I know, Ms. Maitland."

1

The passage can best be described as

A) a comprehensive account of Ms. Maitland's duties as headmistress.

B) an illustration of Ms. Maitland's style of daily management.

C) a warning against romantic and personal attachments in the workplace.

D) a glimpse into the conflicts that burden a modern-day boarding school.

2

The author would most likely agree with which statement about Ms. Maitland?

A) Her stern demeanor is a source of intimidation for her employees.

B) She is suspicious of the motives of her subordinates in the school.

C) She is fair and compassionate in the way she manages her staff.

D) She is perceptive in her assessments of those under her supervision.

3

Which choice provides the best evidence for the answer to the previous question?

A) Lines 2-3 ("Her mood . . . school")

B) Lines 19-20 ("Ms. Maitland . . . eye on")

C) Lines 23-25 ("And since . . . time")

D) Lines 53-54 ("Ms. Maitland . . . manner")

4

As used in line 1, the word "set" most nearly means

A) placed.

B) clenched.

C) mended.

D) formed.

5

The parenthetical statement in lines 16-17 functions to

A) accurately blame family influences for poor academic performance.

B) provide background information on a character who later becomes important.

C) illustrate the sense of personal responsibility that Ms. Maitland feels for all the students in her school.

D) communicate Ms. Maitland's awareness of the absurdity of an earlier remark.

6

It can be inferred from information in the passage that Ms. Maitland assigns Mr. Boyce to the art class mostly because

A) she needs somebody to maintain order.

B) she values his sense of fashion.

C) she wants to distance him from her secretary.

D) she feels a need to humiliate him.

7

Which choice provides the best evidence for the answer to the previous question?

A) Lines 32-33 ("He was . . . jacket")

B) Lines 38-39 ("I have . . . topic")

C) Lines 39-41 ("The bell . . . grateful")

D) Lines 42-43 ("Tim raised . . . adamant")

8

As used in line 49, "thawed" most nearly means

A) tensed.

B) defrosted.

C) relaxed.

D) weakened.

9

Janet's response to Ms. Maitland's observation, "You are looking a little fatigued" (line 57), suggests that

A) Janet feels guilty about her association with Tim Boyce.

B) Janet uses deception to gain an advantage in a challenging situation.

C) Janet feels close enough to Ms. Maitland to disclose her personal activities.

D) Janet takes her job seriously and addresses Ms. Maitland with unwavering respect.

10

The passage most strongly suggests that Ms. Maitland's job duties are

A) diverse.

B) stressful.

C) complicated.

D) predictable.

Questions 11-21 are based on the following passage and supplementary material.

In the passage that follows, the author considers the connections between Japanese urban life and non-traditional forms of art.

As a form of expression, graffiti is famously characterized by outlaw values; after all, even the creation and display of graffiti may counter societal rules or be destructive to
Line property. We see can see this mentality play out in any number
5 of American cities—and, on the other side of the globe, in the metropolises of contemporary Japan. The links between Asian graffiti culture and principles of rebellion are not mere coincidences. After all, the popularization of graffiti in Japan is tied to the influx of hip-hop music, much of it subversive and
10 much of it originating in the United States and Europe.

Yet in the mid 1990s, after the first experiments in Japanese street art had run their course, graffiti in Japan began to establish a foothold in respectable artistic communities. Many artists regarded graffiti as a means of displaying their work in more
15 free and open settings than traditional Japanese painting could provide. This is not to say that graffiti has been universally embraced in Japan. For older Japanese citizens, graffiti continues to recall a gang activity known as "tagging" (the act of marking one's territory using painted slogans or symbols). For this reason,
20 Japanese graffiti still bears the stigma of illegality. Perhaps worse in a country determined to preserve its history, graffiti is associated with the destruction of property. Graffiti, however, also designates and promotes property and culture: rebellious credentials aside, many of the finest Japanese graffiti artists work
25 as private contractors, creating billboards, signs, and community murals. Indeed, the relationship between the Japanese and graffiti is nothing less than paradoxical.

While the most basic function of graffiti is to display artistic talent (or to betray a lack of talent), graffiti itself actually
30 indicates something deeper about the modern Japanese lifestyle: like other Japanese art forms, Japanese graffiti cultivates an awareness of man's place within nature. The colors, shapes, and subjects of graffiti in such cities as Tokyo and Kyoto have been influential in collapsing distinctions between the city and
35 the whole of the living, growing universe. On the most obvious level, Japanese street art is rich in images of plants, animals, and unspoiled landscapes. On a more subtle level, such art reminds us that a city, any city, is an "ecosystem" like any other.

This connection between nature and culture is especially
40 evident in the city of Shibuya, which has been a hub of graffiti activity. The home of the large and well-maintained Yoyogi park, Shibuya is not completely removed from the natural world. Perhaps for this reason, Shibuya's graffiti artists have been especially interested in the reconciliation of natural and
45 manmade forces. In one collaboration, graffiti artists nicknamed

CONTINUE

KAMI, SASU, and KRESS created a mural that shows a dreamlike and dynamic city: flowing blue shapes and a bleak landscape of gray come together in a scene of initial tension and eventual, organic harmony.

50   Such works are natural outgrowths of urban life; moreover, they signify human vitality and beautify otherwise empty landscapes. Graffiti is, thus, useful for the Japanese. That is why it belongs. And the same principle justifies other urban sights that may at first strike Westerners as odd. Large vending

55 machines are found in parks throughout Japan, yet are not seen as unnatural by park visitors. Attitudes could not be more different in the United States: vending machines are wholly of human creation, and therefore should be perceived as out-of-place in predominantly natural spaces. Yet according to

60 Japanese conceptions of nature, these machines blend in because they serve defined functions—functions less glamorous than, but perhaps not too different from, those of the graffiti that beautifies Japanese urban life.

11

The primary purpose of the passage is to

A) indirectly argue that legalized graffiti would beautify American cities.

B) present one country's story as a cautionary tale about the dangers of unregulated public art.

C) explore the unique role of a particular form of expression in Japan.

D) distinguish between graffiti as an art form and graffiti as vandalism.

12

Which of the following best describes the developmental pattern of the passage?

A) A form of art is introduced, its recent history is outlined, and a few contemporary uses are described in detail.

B) A contrast between two countries is investigated, a new interpretation is offered, and proposals for future action are set forward.

C) A hypothesis is developed, a few recent case studies are considered, and old ideas are critiqued and discarded.

D) A misunderstood activity is analyzed, its benefits and drawbacks are assessed, and it is ultimately declared detrimental in most modern contexts.

13

The author of the passage would most likely argue that the primary role of graffiti in Japan is to

A) help artists earn reputations that bolster their more mainstream artistic endeavors.

B) decorate city streets with pleasing images.

C) blur the boundary between urban and natural life.

D) demarcate the territories of rival communities.

Approval of Graffiti as a Valid Art Form Among Japanese Citizens

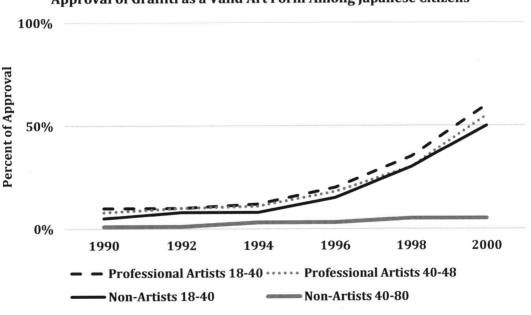

Professional Artists 18-40 · · · · · Professional Artists 40-48
Non-Artists 18-40   Non-Artists 40-80

14

Which choice provides the best evidence for the answer to the previous question?

A) Lines 11-13 ("Yet in . . . communities")
B) Lines 17-19 ("For older . . . symbols")
C) Lines 32-35 ("The colors . . . universe")
D) Lines 52-53 ("Graffiti is . . . belongs")

15

As used in line 36, "rich in" most nearly means

A) prosperous from.
B) plentiful in.
C) subsidized by.
D) overloaded with.

16

The author indicates that graffiti in Japan is

A) anti-consumerist and economically radical.
B) becoming less important now that changing technologies offer new avenues for expression.
C) used for both subversive and commercial causes.
D) immensely popular with the young yet fundamentally educational in intent.

17

Which choice provides the best evidence for the answer to the previous question?

A) Lines 8-10 ("After all . . . Europe")
B) Lines 13-16 ("Many artists . . . provide")
C) Lines 22-26 ("Graffiti, however . . . murals")
D) Lines 53-54 ("And the same . . . as odd")

18

According to the passage, which of the following are viewed as incompatible in the United States?

A) Technology and nature
B) Art and economics
C) Tradition and self-expression
D) Ambition and sensitivity

19

The author discusses vending machines in the final paragraph of this passage in order to demonstrate

A) the vast cultural gulf between Eastern and Western notions of what constitutes useful space.
B) how graffiti combines the natural and the industrial in a manner unfamiliar to Westerners.
C) the extent to which Japanese cities have been destabilized by new merchandising practices.
D) the role of publicly accessible art in the revitalization of blighted urban spaces.

20

It can be inferred from the passage and the graph that before the mid-1990s

A) graffiti was not known to artists in Japan.
B) graffiti artists were mostly small-time criminals.
C) relatively few established Japanese artists practiced graffiti.
D) Japanese graffiti was mostly confined to museums and art galleries.

21

The author would most likely attribute the difference in approval of graffiti among age groups to

A) the earlier association of graffiti with gang behavior.
B) the inability of young people to respect their elders.
C) interest in the intersection between nature and urban life.
D) a growing acceptance of graffiti within artistic communities.

CONTINUE

Test 2

Questions 22-32 are based on the following passage and supplementary material.

Written by a specialist in evolutionary science and animal cognition, this passage considers recent research on bird species from Europe and North America.

In the mythologies of Greece, China, Scandinavia, and the ancient Americas, ravens and their kindred species were regarded as highly intelligent tricksters—a portrayal that has only been backed up by scientific fieldwork. Domesticated ravens are capable of imitating human speech; wild ravens manipulate manmade tools and traps, develop complex strategies to evade predators, and indulge in play and recreation. (Ravens in snowy areas will lie on their abdomens and "sled" down hills and off roofs.) As understood today, bird intelligence involves much more than simple tricks and parroted phrases. Traits such as anxiety, empathy, and recognition are in fact traits that we humans share with avian life all over the planet.

Nor are the emblematic ravens the only birds with such impressive capabilities. As new research has demonstrated, acute perception and social coordination are traits that ravens share with the other, seldom-mythologized birds in their family, including the reclusive Siberian Jay.

In October of 2015, a group of researchers from the University of Zurich published evidence of one of this raven relative's remarkable abilities—the Siberian Jay's aptitude for recognizing distant relatives within its own species. Such an aptitude is rare among animals: according to *Science Daily*, "in few mammal, bird, and fish species, individuals can recognize unfamiliar siblings," to say nothing of more distant kin. However, it could be a potent survival tool. Because Siberian Jays with the same bloodline travel together and gravitate to localized and limited food sources, such as mammal carcasses, these Jays would have good reason to drive away unrelated and potentially disruptive fellows Jays.

The aggressively territorial nature of the Siberian Jay—a monogamous bird which is intensely protective of its immediate family—was exploited by the University of Zurich team. Throughout the study, the researchers worked with a Jay population located in Northern Sweden. For identification purposes, small metal leg rings were used to tag the Jays; for the purposes of tracing lineage, blood samples were obtained and catalogued. The researchers, moreover, did not wait for the Jays to find their food at random. Instead, the team rigged up feeding stations throughout the Jays' forest habitat, luring the Jays with slices of pig fat. In the course of three years of careful fieldwork (1999, 2008, and 2009), typical patterns of interaction among the Jays became evident. It turns out that the typical Siberian Jay dislikes its distant relatives, but dislikes completely unrelated Jays even more.

As stated in the article that resulted from this research, the closely-related groups of Jays drove away outsiders (or "immigrants") in "a graded manner, in that they chased most intensely the immigrant group members that were genetically the least related." The reasons why Jays would benefit from this ability are clear, according to team leader Michael Griesser. In his words, "it's a selective advantage to share food only with close relatives and not very distant or unrelated individuals." More mysterious (and not a primary consideration of the study in any case) is *how* the Jays can make such fine distinctions.

While Griesser's study does address only one bird species, its results should make us wary of drawing quick and easy conclusions about how birds think. The temptation, especially when evaluating intriguingly adept species such as jays and ravens, is to assume that bird intelligence is simply a displaced form of human intelligence. Birds may indeed think in some of the same ways that we humans do, but maybe the ways they think differently and perceive better are the factors that truly define bird intelligence. After all, what are the chances that you could recognize a relative ten times removed?

Percentage of Distant Relatives Successfully Identified

Closeness of Family Relation Between Test Group Birds and Immigrant Birds

Bird Species	One Remove	Two Removes	Three Removes	Four Removes	Five Removes	Six Removes	Seven Removes
Raven	80%	75%	70%	25%	20%	5%	0%
Siberian Jay	95%	90%	90%	85%	80%	80%	75%
Magpie	85%	75%	60%	60%	35%	10%	10%
Blue Jay	65%	50%	40%	25%	10%	0%	0%

CONTINUE

22

Which of the following best describes the developmental pattern of the passage?

A) An experiment is described, its results are listed, and possible improvements to the methodology are suggested.

B) A series of facts is presented, a recent inquiry is explained, and an important qualification is stated.

C) A contrast between species is introduced, a loosely related research project is described, and the need for further research is emphasized.

D) A common source of confusion is introduced, an initial solution is offered, and a broader set of principles is outlined.

23

As used in line 12, "share with" most nearly means

A) have in common with.

B) partake of alongside.

C) appreciate because of.

D) allocate to.

24

In the passage, the raven is mentioned as an example of a bird that

A) has learned complex behaviors by observing humans.

B) has few natural predators and can thrive in ecosystems dominated by humans

C) is much more prominent in human culture than the Siberian Jay.

D) is mistakenly seen as more intelligent than the Siberian Jay.

25

Which choice provides the best evidence for the answer to the previous question?

A) Lines 4-8 ("Domesticated . . . recreation")

B) Lines 11-13 ("Traits such . . . planet")

C) Lines 15-18 ("As new . . . Siberian Jay")

D) Lines 58-61 ("The temptation . . . intelligence")

26

The passage identifies which of the following as an expected trait of Siberian Jays?

A) Hostility to unrelated and outsider Jays

B) Adaptability to harsh weather

C) Indifference to humans

D) Formation of multi-generational family groups

27

The most likely purpose of the parenthetical information in lines 54-55 is to

A) foreshadow Michael Griesser's next project.

B) point out an intended limitation.

C) question an earlier assumption.

D) refute a common argument.

28

As used in line 57, "quick and easy" most nearly means

A) effortless and entertaining.

B) alluring yet dishonest.

C) insufficiently rigorous.

D) surprisingly efficient.

29

According to the passage, the study undertaken by the University of Zurich team is significant because

A) its methodologies can be used to study bird species other than the Siberian Jay.

B) it settles earlier disputes about why the Siberian Jay evolved its recognition abilities.

C) it helped scientists understand how bird species in harsh climates locate food and other resources.

D) its findings have broader implications for how bird intelligence is commonly understood.

CONTINUE

30

Which choice provides the best evidence for the answer to the previous question?

A) Lines 19-22 ("In October . . . species")

B) Lines 26-30 ("Because Siberian . . . Jays")

C) Lines 50-51 ("The reasons . . . Griesser")

D) Lines 56-58 ("While Griesser's . . . think")

31

Does the table substantiate the passage's claims about "the Siberian Jay's aptitude for recognizing distant relatives within its own species" (lines 21-22)?

A) Yes, because the recognition rate among Siberian Jays is high even for far-removed relatives.

B) Yes, because only Siberian Jays are capable of reliably recognizing far-removed relatives.

C) No, because magpies can also recognize a large number of relatives at three or four removes.

D) No, because the data disprove the passage's claims about the similarities between ravens and Siberian Jays.

32

According to the data in the table, the greatest decrease in success rate is experienced by

A) Ravens, between three and four removes.

B) Ravens, between four and seven removes.

C) Blue Jays, between one and three removes.

D) Blue Jays, between three and four removes.

Questions 33-42 are based on the following passage.

This selection is an excerpt from Alexis de Tocqueville's *Democracy in America* (1835-1840), a book that considers the ideals behind early American society and politics.

I think that in no country in the civilized world has less attention been paid to philosophy than in the United States. The Americans have no philosophical school of their own, and they
Line care but little for all the schools into which Europe is divided,
5 the very names of which are scarcely known to them.
    Yet it is easy to perceive that almost all the inhabitants of the United States use their minds in the same manner, and direct them according to the same rules; that is to say, without ever having taken the trouble to define the rules, they have a
10 philosophical method common to the whole people.
    To evade the bondage of system and habit, of family maxims, class opinions, and, in some degree, of national prejudices; to accept tradition only as a means of information, and existing facts only as a lesson to be used in doing otherwise
15 and doing better; to seek the reason of things for oneself, and in oneself alone; to tend to results without being bound to means, and to strike through the form to the substance—such are the principal characteristics of what I shall call the philosophical method of the Americans.
20   But if I go further and seek among these characteristics the principal one, which includes almost all the rest, I discover that in most of the operations of the mind each American appeals only to the individual effort of his own understanding.
    America is therefore one of the countries where the
25 precepts of Descartes are least studied and are best applied. Nor is this surprising. The Americans do not read the works of Descartes, because their social condition deters them from speculative studies; but they follow his maxims, because this same social condition naturally disposes their minds to adopt
30 them.
    In the midst of the continual movement that agitates a democratic community, the tie that unites one generation to another is relaxed or broken; every man there readily loses all trace of the ideas of his forefathers or takes no care about them.
35   Men living in this state of society cannot derive their belief from the opinions of the class to which they belong; for, so to speak, there are no longer any classes, or those which still exist are composed of such mobile elements that the body can never exercise any real control over its members.
40   As to the influence which the intellect of one man may have on that of another, it must necessarily be very limited in a country where the citizens, placed on an equal footing, are all closely seen by one another; and where, as no signs of incontestable greatness or superiority are perceived in any one
45 of them, they are constantly brought back to their own reason

CONTINUE

as the most obvious and proximate source of truth. It is not
only confidence in this or that man which is destroyed, but
the disposition to trust the authority of any man whatsoever.
Everyone shuts himself up tightly within himself and insists
50 upon judging the world from there.

The practice of Americans leads their minds to other
habits, to fixing the standard of their judgment in themselves
alone. As they perceive that they succeed in resolving without
assistance all the little difficulties which their practical life
55 presents, they readily conclude that everything in the world
may be explained, and that nothing in it transcends the limits of
the understanding. Thus they fall to denying what they cannot
comprehend, which leaves them but little faith for whatever
is extraordinary and an almost insurmountable distaste for
60 whatever is supernatural. As it is on their own testimony that
they are accustomed to rely, they like to discern the object
which engages their attention with extreme clearness; they
therefore strip off as much as possible all that covers it; they
rid themselves of whatever separates them from it, they
65 remove whatever conceals it from sight, in order to view it
more closely and in the broad light of day. This disposition of
mind soon leads them to condemn forms, which they regard
as useless and inconvenient veils placed between them and the
truth.

33

Which of the following statements is supported by the
passage?

A) While Americans may not have a definitive philosophy,
they all adhere to the same basic school of thought.

B) Americans are unpredictable and stubborn individuals
who do not listen to reason.

C) All Americans strictly observe and study the same
singular philosophy.

D) Every individual American has his or her own moral
philosophy.

34

Which choice provides the best evidence for the answer to
the previous question?

A) Lines 3-5 ("they care . . . them")

B) Lines 8-10 ("without ever . . . people")

C) Lines 24-25 ("America is . . . applied")

D) Lines 35-36 ("Men living . . . belong")

35

The list of attributes in lines 11-19 serves to

A) catalog long-standing disagreements between
Americans.

B) illustrate the various attitudes of those who settled in
America.

C) provide examples of mindsets that the author disputes
later in the passage.

D) show what philosophical principles are common among
Americans.

36

Of all the philosophies common to America society, the
main one which incorporates the rest is that

A) Americans' schools of philosophical thought have
strong European influences.

B) Americans rely on a very controversial and provocative
way of thinking.

C) Americans only support that which they are able to
understand.

D) Americans reject all ideas that are not overtly patriotic.

37

As used in line 31, "agitates" most nearly means

A) drives.

B) bothers.

C) troubles.

D) disturbs.

38

Based on the information in the passage, Americans in a
democratic society base their judgments on

A) what other people tell them is right and wrong.

B) religious texts and teachings on ethical responsibility.

C) various European philosophical teachings.

D) their own perspectives and sense of reason.

CONTINUE

39

In lines 51-57 ("The practice . . . understanding"), Tocqueville describes Americans as being

A) fundamentally patriotic.

B) ultimately myopic.

C) independent in mindset.

D) averse to contemplation.

40

According to Tocqueville, Americans reject

A) everything that is not considered American.

B) what they cannot understand or explain.

C) all opinions that are not their own.

D) those who are immigrants to America.

41

Which choice provides the best evidence for the answer to the previous question?

A) Lines 26-28 ("The Americans . . . maxims")

B) Lines 40-43 ("As to the . . . another")

C) Lines 57-60 ("Thus they . . . supernatural")

D) Lines 66-69 ("This disposition . . . truth")

42

As used in line 65, "remove" most nearly means

A) relocate.

B) purge.

C) abolish.

D) eject.

Questions 43-52 are based on the following passages.

The two passages below discuss the acquisition of language by infants. Passage 1 is adapted from a 2002 book on infant psychology. Passage 2 was written by a science journalist in 2004.

Passage 1

From the very moment we come into this world, we find ourselves adrift in a sea of language. If it were possible to look back on our first few moments of life, we would likely
Line recall a cacophony of unknown sounds, spoken by our nearest
5 relatives. These strange sounds, incomprehensible to us at first, miraculously begin to take on both shape and meaning. In time, we learn to associate the word "clock" with the round object with two hands that hangs upon the wall, while "cloud" comes to stand for that white ball of cotton up in the sky. This process
10 of language acquisition is so natural and organic that we scarcely notice its occurrence at all. By the age of seven or eight, most of us have experienced such total language acquisition that, by the time we reach adulthood, we find it nearly impossible to conceive of a world without language. We have simply become
15 so accustomed to seeing our world through the veil of our mother tongue that the world as an "undivided canvas"—that is, the world as perceived by an infant—has been all but lost from memory.

In acquiring language, we gain the convenience and the
20 expediency of a shared and common lexicon, while losing the holistic view of the world that is one aspect of infancy. This is because our language acts as a knife, splitting the world neatly into subjects and objects—"I" as opposed to "you," "this" as opposed to "that," "us" as opposed to "them." Thus, we
25 come see the world as a random jumble of distinct objects, not because this is how the world truly is, but because this is the best response to the world that our language can muster—and it is an inadequate response at best. Is it a fact that my neighbor, the sun, and the air around us are all quite distinct and separable things,
30 when in fact the sun is at all times heating the air, which is in turn being inhaled by my neighbor, only to be absorbed by his lungs and circulated by his blood? When we truly consider the diverse and nuanced interrelationships in the world around us, we begin to see that our language is capable of describing things
35 only piecemeal.

Passage 2

To long for the golden days of our youth is perhaps natural, but if this yearning is indulged for too long it becomes an exercise in futility. One would think that scientists, being some of the brightest and most pragmatic individuals among us, would
40 most especially agree with this sentiment. Yet in the field of psychology, there is a small but vociferous group of researchers who seem to view our very first few moments of life as a kind of

paradisaical state, as the very pinnacle of human experience—if only we could remember it. According to these "experts," it is
45 only in the pure, unadulterated consciousness of our infancy that we can experience the world as a unified whole, or "as it really is." It is on account of this process of language acquisition, so the researchers claim, that our words come to surround us like the curved and crooked mirrors of a funhouse, distorting our
50 ability to see anything clearly.

Such sentiments are neither new nor remarkable in the field of psychology. Over a century ago, Sigmund Freud himself commented on the infantile consciousness, which he referred to as the "oceanic state." "That feeling of oneness with
55 the universe," wrote Freud, in his seminal text *Civilization and Its Discontents*, "sounds . . . like another way taken by the ego of denying the dangers it sees threatening in the external world." According to Freud himself, the "oceanic state" is a case of the ego in denial—not unlike the state of mind of the current crop of
60 researchers, who denounce language as the cause of all our woes. In their very view of the matter, they deny some very basic facts of reality—namely, that if it were not for those language-using, "fallen" adults who nurtured us from the very first day of life, the "oceanic state" that these researchers praise would hardly
65 be sustainable at all. To long for the days of our pre-linguistic infancy is to go against a very natural and ordered flow.

43

Which statement best describes the relationship between the two passages?

A) Passage 1 describes a phenomenon that Passage 2 finds to be a cause of concern.

B) Passage 1 discusses the advantages and disadvantages of a process that Passage 2 examines in detail.

C) Passage 2 predicts the outcome of an intellectual movement that is analyzed in Passage 1.

D) Passage 2 dismisses a viewpoint that Passage 1 considers to be partially valid.

44

The author of Passage 1 refers to the "clock" (line 7) and the "cloud" (line 8) primarily to

A) pinpoint concepts that can be understood regardless of language.

B) present a contrast between natural and man-made aspects of the world.

C) cite examples of sounds to which we have assigned names and meanings.

D) support the argument that language acquisition can have adverse effects.

45

It can be inferred that the author of Passage 1 views language acquisition as

A) convenient and liberating.

B) unnecessary and harmful.

C) alarming yet systematic.

D) useful yet limiting.

46

Which choice provides the best evidence for the answer to the previous question?

A) Lines 2-5 ("If it . . . relatives")

B) Lines 5-6 ("These strange . . . meaning")

C) Lines 19-21 ("In acquiring . . . infancy")

D) Lines 21-23 ("This is . . . objects")

47

The statement in lines 21-24 ("This is . . . them") of Passage 1 has primarily which effect?

A) It employs figurative language to illustrate a concept.

B) It illustrates the thought process behind the author's argument.

C) It provides evidence for the thesis in the first paragraph.

D) It offers an example of the advantages of language use.

48

Which choice provides the best evidence that the author of Passage 1 would agree to some extent with the claim attributed to the "experts" in lines 44-47 of Passage 2?

A) Lines 6-9 ("In time . . . sky")

B) Lines 11-14 ("By the . . . language")

C) Lines 28-32 ("Is it a . . . blood?")

D) Lines 32-35 ("When we . . . piecemeal")

CONTINUE

49

As used in line 49, "crooked" most nearly means

A) corrupt.

B) warped.

C) disfigured.

D) suspicious.

50

As used in line 59, "crop" most nearly means

A) group.

B) yield.

C) supply.

D) portion.

51

The author of Passage 2 reacts to the apparent desirability of the "oceanic state" (line 54) with

A) wholehearted assent.

B) cautious acceptance.

C) qualified doubt.

D) complete disagreement.

52

On which of the following points would the authors of both passages most likely agree?

A) It is only when we forgo language completely that we are able to view the world as it truly is.

B) The process of language acquisition can feel both innate and organic.

C) Wishing to experience life as we understood it as infants is reasonable and natural.

D) Language acquisition is a difficult and complex but rewarding process.

STOP

If you finish before time is called, you may check your work on this section only.

Do not turn to any other section.

Answer Key: TEST 2

Test 2

PASSAGE 1
Fiction

1. B
2. D
3. C
4. B
5. D
6. A
7. C
8. C
9. C
10. A

PASSAGE 2
Social Science

11. C
12. A
13. C
14. C
15. B
16. C
17. C
18. A
19. B
20. C
21. A

PASSAGE 3
Natural Science 1

22. B
23. A
24. C
25. C
26. A
27. B
28. C
29. D
30. D
31. A
32. A

PASSAGE 4
Global Conversation

33. A
34. B
35. D
36. C
37. A
38. D
39. C
40. B
41. C
42. B

PASSAGE 5
Natural Science 2

43. D
44. C
45. D
46. C
47. A
48. D
49. B
50. A
51. D
52. B

Once you have determined how many questions
you answered correctly, consult the chart on Page 174
to determine your **SAT Reading Test score.**

Please visit **ies2400.com/answers** for answer explanations.

Post-Test Analysis

This post-test analysis is essential if you want to see an improvement on your next test. Possible reasons for errors on the five passages in this test are listed here. Place check marks next to the types of errors that pertain to you, or write your own types of errors in the blank spaces.

TIMING AND ACCURACY

◇ Spent too long reading individual passages
◇ Spent too long answering each question
◇ Spent too long on a few difficult questions
◇ Felt rushed and made silly mistakes or random errors
◇ Unable to work quickly using textual evidence and POE
Other: _____

APPROACHING THE PASSAGES AND QUESTIONS

◇ Unable to effectively grasp a passage's tone or style
◇ Unable to effectively grasp a passage's topic or stance
◇ Did not understand the context of line references
◇ Did not eliminate false answers using strong evidence
◇ Answered questions using first impressions instead of POE
◇ Answered questions without checking or inserting final answer
◇ Eliminated correct answer during POE
◇ Consistent trouble with Word in Context vocabulary
◇ Consistent trouble with Command of Evidence questions
◇ Consistent trouble with passage comparison questions
Other: _____

> **Use this form** to better analyze your performance. If you don't understand why you made errors, there is no way that you can correct them!

FICTION: # CORRECT _____ # WRONG _____ # OMITTED _____

◇ Could not grasp the roles and attitudes of major characters
◇ Could not grasp the significance of particular scenes or images
◇ Difficulty understanding the author's style and language
◇ Difficulty understanding the tone, theme, and structure of the passage as a whole
Other: _____

SOCIAL SCIENCE AND
GLOBAL CONVERSATION: # CORRECT _____ # WRONG _____ # OMITTED _____

◇ Unable to grasp the overall argument or thesis of an individual passage
◇ Unable to work effectively with the specific data or evidence in a passage
◇ Unable to respond effectively to tone, structure, and vocabulary
◇ Difficulty working with the graphics and graphic questions in a Social Science passage
◇ Difficulty understanding the logic or methodology of a Social Science passage
◇ Difficulty with the style and language of a Global Conversation passage
◇ Difficulty with the main historical and political concepts of a Global Conversation passage
Other: _____

NATURAL SCIENCE: # CORRECT _____ # WRONG _____ # OMITTED _____

◇ Unable to grasp the overall argument or thesis of an individual passage
◇ Unable to work effectively with the specific data or evidence in a passage
◇ Unable to respond effectively to tone, structure, and vocabulary
◇ Difficulty understanding the significance of the theories or experiments presented
◇ Difficulty working with the graphics and graphic questions
Other: _____

TEST 3

Reading Test
65 MINUTES, 52 QUESTIONS

Turn to Section 1 of your answer sheet to answer the questions in this section.

Each passage or pair of passages below is followed by a number of questions. After reading each passage or pair, choose the best answer to each question based on what is stated or implied in the passage or passages and in any accompanying graphics (such as a table or graph).

Questions 1-10 are based on the following passage.

The passage that follows is adapted from a work of historical fiction written in 2013.

William the Miller was neither the poorest nor the wickedest man in the village. However, if anyone inquired about the use he made of his miller's thumb when he pressed it
Line casually on the scales whilst measuring out flour, he would grin
5 and shrug his shoulders. "We all have a choice in life. Take it or leave it."

William's wife, Abigail, approved. She had been just eighteen when William had approached her parents to ask their permission to court her. They had been delighted, and when
10 he had offered her a place in his heart and a sparkling, jeweled bracelet, Abigail had been delighted too. Her disappointed other suitors had sulked a while, and her closest friends had pointed out that William was twenty years older than she; nonetheless, she had defied these reservations and donned the gown with the
15 steeple head-dress that came with her elevated position in life. The tradesmen now gave her precedence, no matter how long the queue, and, whenever she went to church, the other village women stood aside so she could enter first.

It was in church that she first noticed Absalom. He was
20 a poor student, newly come to the town, and on holy days he helped the priest by collecting the weekly tithe from the parishioners. His coat was patched but his eyes were of the deepest blue Abigail had ever encountered.

Waiting by the church door while William chatted with
25 the priest, Abigail considered Absalom. He was about the same age as she. She then turned and eyed William critically as he lumbered up the aisle towards her. His hair was graying and he had put on much weight since their marriage. No doubt he would sink into a doze before the fire after supper. She sighed,
30 and then caressed the gold bangle on her wrist, a birthday gift from William.

"You saw that new young lad in church?"

William's rough voice broke her reverie. She looked at him, her cheeks burning.
35 "What new lad? Oh yes, he took the tithe. I didn't quite notice him."

"You must have been the only female in the church that didn't! Priest says that the lad needs a place to live. Told him, the boy could have a room at ours. He's paying, of course. He'll
40 be good money for me and some company for you, when I am working."

The color in her cheeks retreated. "Are you sure? People might talk."

"Nonsense! You're the Miller's wife. They know your
45 worth." He paused. "I know your worth. Like Caesar's wife, as they say, you are above suspicion."*

Abigail dropped her eyes. "As you say," she replied demurely.

So Absalom moved into the loft at the mill. At first, Abigail
50 was unnerved by this nearness, but it was not long before she found that it was a boon to have Absalom about the grounds when William was not there. He claimed that he was studying, at which she laughed, for she saw no books. She soon got into the routine of preparing his favorite eggs and bits of pickled beef
55 exactly on time for his morning descent from the loft, long after William's departure for work. Absalom had a healthy appetite. "William is a very lucky man!" he would exclaim, and Abigail would blush and giggle and give him a clip on the ear, just as she had once done with her younger brother.
60 Then, one warm morning—it was a Monday, she remembered later—Absalom seized her hand and kissed it. She looked into those deep blue eyes. There was a stillness that seemed tangible.

CONTINUE ➤

She withdrew her hand. "No."

65   The world came rushing back. He looked at her, astonished and wounded. She stepped back behind the table. She could hear the chickens clucking in the yard outside. She looked around and saw the sack of corn that was their feed.

    "Take this and feed them, will you?" she said, and gave
70 him a maternal smile. "Caesar's wife," she added, by way of explanation. "We all have a choice to make in life. And when we do, then we keep to it or leave it."

    Absalom nodded slowly and went to feed the chickens.

* "Caesar's wife must be above suspicion," Roman proverb

1

As used in line 14, "defied" most nearly means

A) questioned.
B) denigrated.
C) disregarded.
D) rebelled against.

2

It can most reasonably be inferred from the passage that Abigail chose William because

A) the marriage raised her position in society.
B) William was well-liked in the village.
C) she felt that marriage was inevitable for her.
D) William charmed her with his wit.

3

Which choice provides the best evidence for the answer to the previous question?

A) Lines 7-9 ("She had . . . her")
B) Lines 13-15 ("nonetheless . . . in life")
C) Lines 22-23 ("His coat . . . encountered")
D) Lines 29-31 ("She sighed . . . William")

4

The author uses the word "critically" in line 26 to show that Abigail

A) sees William as less attractive than Absalom.
B) has hidden complaints about how William treats her.
C) is an unnecessarily judgmental wife.
D) no longer wants to be seen in public with William.

5

The contrast between Abigail's cheeks in line 34 and in line 42 shows that Abigail's emotions change from

A) mortified to complacent.
B) surprised to furious.
C) indifferent to critical.
D) embarrassed to apprehensive.

6

What is most reasonable to infer about William's attitude toward Abigail?

A) William believes that Abigail is indebted to him.
B) William trusts that Abigail will be faithful to him.
C) William is certain that Abigail is lying to him.
D) William doubts that Abigail will keep Absalom company.

7

Which choice provides the best evidence for the answer to the previous question?

A) Lines 37-38 ("You must . . . didn't!")
B) Lines 39-41 ("He'll be . . . working")
C) Lines 45-46 ("I know . . . suspicion")
D) Lines 47-48 ("Abigail . . . demurely")

CONTINUE ➡

8

As used in line 70, the phrase "a maternal smile" mainly serves to

A) suggest that Abigail used to be close to her brother.

B) indicate that Abigail no longer has a romantic interest in Absalom.

C) insinuate that Abigail wants to be a mother.

D) imply that Abigail wants Absalom to continue living at the mill.

9

As used in line 61, "seized" most nearly means

A) clutched.

B) captivated.

C) overpowered.

D) afflicted.

10

Abigail's comment in lines 71-72 ("We all . . . leave it") serves as a

A) foreshadowing of a later conflict.

B) reference to a historical event involving Caesar.

C) connection to a previously mentioned idea.

D) transition to a discussion of new obligations.

Questions 11-21 are based on the following passages.

The following two passages consider the theories developed by Charles Darwin (1809-1882) and their application to the social and natural sciences. The first passage is taken from an essay on the history of ideas, while the second is adapted from a recent article by a business journalist.

Passage 1

Throughout the history of science, the most monumental discoveries are often described as "groundbreaking." Such indeed was Charles Darwin's seminal work, *On the Origin of*
Line *the Species* (1859). It was in this text that Darwin first elucidated
5 his theory of "natural selection"—that is, the gradual biological process by which the most successfully adapted members of a species pass along their genetic information through reproduction. Over time, the population of a species will change to show increased numbers of optimized traits. Responding to
10 this phenomenon, biologist Herbert Spencer coined the term "survival of the fittest" to describe Darwin's theory.

In the century and a half since, the theory of survival of the fittest has influenced the thinking of experts in fields as diverse as finance and sociology. For instance, Darwin's theory
15 provided physical, concrete evidence for the abstract theories proposed by economist Adam Smith a century earlier. According to Smith, the ideal economic environment for a society is free-market capitalism, a structure in which open competition among producers yields the best products for consumers, manufactured
20 and sold at the lowest possible prices. Smith even described the marriage of supply and demand in the marketplace as something that occurred quite naturally and organically—as if the entire process were orchestrated by an "invisible hand." When Darwin came along, his theory of how nature selects
25 the fittest individuals, thereby yielding the strongest and most robust populations, proved to be a strong justification for Smith's economic teachings.

Of course, the corollary to "survival of the fittest" is that the weaker populations in nature will not survive over the long
30 term. "Natural Selection," wrote Darwin, "almost inevitably causes extinction of the less improved forms of life." Is it any surprise then, as we look around the world today, that capitalism has flourished across the globe—even in countries that once had purely communist economies, such as Russia and China?
35 Even now, Darwin and Smith reign supreme in the realm of economics.

Passage 2

Every now and then, I do a little digging online and try to find out what has happened to the people I knew in college. I'm mostly curious whether my prophecies for their
40 careers and successes have in any way come true. Often, my

CONTINUE

prognostications are stunningly wrong. I recently looked up one of my highest-achieving classmates, who graduated with an honors degree in physics and mathematics, then earned his doctorate in the second of these disciplines. Now, he works as a
45 teacher in a primary school: a comfortable life, but not the future of earth-shattering discovery that I had so confidently predicted. I also recently looked up a few of my dorm-mates from freshman year, particularly two carefree young men who enjoyed sneaking oranges out of the cafeteria and using them to play baseball on a
50 nearby athletic field. Today, one is a successful corporate lawyer, while the other owns a popular chain of Italian restaurants. I wonder if either remembers those oranges.

How strange this all seems, from the perspective of classic economic theory. In college, many of us are taught that the
55 modern world is dictated by "social Darwinism," "survival of the fittest," "the strong against the weak." These ideas aren't unrealistic clichés, but they aren't neatly applicable to the modern job market. If they were, I could have determined my classmates' futures as easily as Darwin himself determined
60 which birds and which reptiles were best suited to which environmental conditions. It just is not so; in truth, the preferences of employers, businessmen, and deal-makers can be absolutely inscrutable. Traits that are typically marks of the "weak"—an easygoing temperament, an irresponsible sense of
65 humor—can sometimes seal an interview or make a career.

The cases I have considered may seem small and, frankly, weird. Still, what are we to make of the many international businesses that seem ready to self-destruct but somehow thrive? How do we explain corporate behemoths such as Amazon.com,
70 a company that has not until recently made a steady profit but is still valued at almost $300 billion? Again, "survival of the fittest" posits that the market is guided by an "invisible hand," which supposedly maintains a logical balance of power. The way I see it, the owner of that invisible hand must be blind, or insane, or
75 possessed of a devious sense of humor.

11

Which statement best describes the relationship between the passages?

A) Passage 2 relates a personal anecdote that supports the claims put forth in Passage 1.

B) Passage 2 questions the validity of a theory that Passage 1 presents in a positive light.

C) Passage 2 argues against the practicality of a proposal suggested in Passage 1.

D) Passage 2 offers possible solutions to a dilemma that Passage 1 examines in depth.

12

The primary purpose of the first paragraph of Passage 1 (lines 1-11) is to

A) describe the life and work of an important and respected scientist.

B) begin an extended metaphor that will continue to the end of the passage.

C) provide an overview of a theory that will later be discussed in different contexts.

D) present a thesis that will be explored further as the passage progresses.

13

As used in line 18, "open" most nearly means

A) unrestricted.

B) exposed.

C) public.

D) accessible.

14

According to the author of Passage 1, capitalism

A) is a legitimate system in theory but has significant flaws in practice.

B) is a necessary evil that must be allowed in order to ensure economic progress.

C) is a popular system that must nonetheless undergo reform.

D) is premised on the idea that different options can optimize results.

15

Which choice provides the best evidence for the answer to the previous question?

A) Lines 14-16 ("Darwin's . . . earlier")

B) Lines 16-20 ("According . . . prices")

C) Lines 20-22 ("Smith . . . organically")

D) Lines 24-27 ("When . . . teachings")

16

How do the two passages differ in their descriptions of the "invisible hand"?

A) The author of Passage 1 treats the invisible hand as an abstract concept, while the author of Passage 2 argues that the invisible hand is present in society.

B) The author of Passage 1 dismisses the invisible hand as an impractical construct, while the author of Passage 2 endorses it as a necessity.

C) The author of Passage 1 questions the relevance of the invisible hand to economics, while the author of Passage 2 criticizes the absurdity of such applications.

D) The author of Passage 1 presents the invisible hand in relation to Darwin's theory, while the author of Passage 2 is skeptical of the concept's soundness.

17

The first paragraph of Passage 2 (lines 37-52) is primarily concerned with establishing a contrast between

A) ambition and self-satisfaction.

B) technology and contemplation.

C) innocence and cleverness.

D) assumption and reality.

18

As used in line 63, "marks" most nearly means

A) vestiges.

B) characteristics.

C) symbols.

D) flaws.

19

The author of Passage 2 responds to the "survival of the fittest" theory by

A) indicating that the implementation of the theory might work in some circumstances but not in others.

B) questioning the logic behind the ideology and suggesting that some of the premises are irrational.

C) expressing strong discomfort about the possible ethical consequences of putting the theory into practice.

D) describing first-hand experiences that further substantiate the argument presented in Passage 1.

20

Which choice provides the best evidence for the answer to the previous question?

A) Lines 40-41 ("Often . . . wrong")

B) Lines 44-46 ("Now . . . predicted")

C) Lines 56-58 ("These . . . market")

D) Lines 61-63 ("the preferences . . . inscrutable")

21

The main purpose of each passage is to

A) discuss the application of Darwin's theories to fields such as economics and the social sciences.

B) take a position on the increasing popularity of Darwin's ideas among prominent historians.

C) document the history of Darwin's theories and the different interpretations that they have received.

D) compare various political and social theories and how they have been adopted by policymakers.

CONTINUE

Questions 22-32 are based on the following passage and supplementary material.

This excerpt from a 2015 journal article explains a recently-observed phenomenon in cell biology.

Research by a team of scientists based at the University of Texas has uncovered a surprising way to stimulate the development of healthy fat in humans; long-term, the team's
Line findings may have implications for the development of
5 weight-loss medication. These scientists, led by geriatrician Labros Sidossis, found that the kind of stress that accompanies massive third-degree burns may induce the human body to convert normal fat cells into brown fat, which burns calories at a higher rate. If future research can determine how and why
10 the body accomplishes this conversion, it may be possible to develop drugs that induce artificial yet remarkably rapid fat-burning in obese patients.

White adipose tissue—normal, white fat—accounts for most of the fat in the bodies of most mammals. Small mammals
15 and newborn humans, however, have a high proportion of brown fat. The key difference between the two, and the factor that has led scientists and physicians to believe that brown fat has potential to combat obesity, is that brown fat contains a surfeit of mitochondria: the structures within body cells that are
20 responsible for producing energy. This means that brown fat burns more calories and releases more heat when it burns. After all, the function of naturally-occurring brown fat is to generate heat in small animals, or in human infants who do not yet have the ability to shiver.

25 The research undertaken by Sidossis's team began with the observation that patients with severe, widespread burns needed to consume more calories each day in order to maintain their weight. To determine where these calories were going, the team studied the fat cells of 48 severe burn patients at a hospital in
30 Galveston, Texas, throughout their treatment. The researchers then collected fat samples in the first few days of the patients' admission and in the weeks that followed as the patients began the recovery process. Analysis of the samples revealed that what was once white adipose tissue had "browned," acquiring
35 many characteristics similar to brown fat, including its ability to burn calories at a high rate.

To explain this observation, the first to confirm that humans can produce brown fat later in life, Sidossis said: "We think that in these patients who have lost much of their skin,
40 which normally helps keep us warm, white fat is turning into brown fat in an effort to increase the ability of the body to produce heat." Whatever the reason for this conversion, on average these patients were burning an extra 263 calories each day. This calorie burn is less than that observed in "native"
45 brown fat, yet still represents over ten percent of a standard 2,000 calorie per day diet. Over time, such gains in caloric expenditure could lead to significant weight loss.

Of course, we are still a long way away from the practical application of these findings. (As any sane medical
50 practitioner will tell you, massive third-degree burns are unlikely to be approved as a treatment for obesity anytime soon.) Rather, this research indicates the possibility of converting white fat into brown and reveals something about the conditions that catalyze such a conversion; maybe, this
55 research also points the way to future inquiries, which may lead to the pharmacological stimulation of this notable fat-burning process. As Sidossis said, this "proof of concept" is just the beginning: "the next step is to find the mechanism."

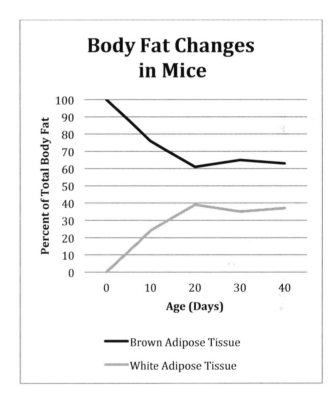

Body Fat Changes in Mice

22

The primary purpose of the passage is to

A) suggest one potential application of a discovery.

B) describe the details of a new technological advancement.

C) discuss the positive effects of an otherwise tragic occurrence.

D) question the relationship between two fields of study.

23

The information in the passage indicates that

A) brown adipose tissue is superior to white adipose tissue.

B) adults possess the capacity to produce brown adipose tissue without the aid of medication.

C) small mammals require higher body temperatures than large ones do.

D) white adipose tissue accounts for a relatively small percentage of adult body fat.

24

Which choice provides the best evidence for the answer to the previous question?

A) Lines 5-9 ("These scientists . . . rate")

B) Lines 20-21 ("This means . . . burns")

C) Lines 21-24 ("After all . . . shiver")

D) Lines 26-28 ("patients . . . weight")

25

Which choice best describes the author's attitude towards the research he presents in the passage?

A) convinced of its accuracy and certain of its significance.

B) pleased with its conclusions and optimistic about its implications.

C) unaware of its shortcomings but skeptical of its importance.

D) unabashedly critical of both its motives and practical uses.

26

Which choice provides the best evidence for the answer to the previous question?

A) Lines 1-3 ("Research . . . humans")

B) Lines 33-36 ("Analysis of . . . rate")

C) Lines 52-55 ("Rather, this . . . inquiries")

D) Line 58 ("the next . . . mechanism")

27

As used in line 36, "burn" most nearly means

A) waste.

B) heat.

C) damage.

D) use.

28

The most likely purpose of the parenthetical information in lines 49-52 is to

A) advocate for the feasibility of a discovery's applications.

B) provide a humorous aside to highlight the absurdity of Sidossis' conclusion.

C) emphasize that the research cited has not yet led to practical measures.

D) caution against a disastrous but nevertheless tempting course of action.

CONTINUE

29

As used in line 56, "stimulation" most nearly means

A) excitement.

B) induction.

C) acceleration.

D) inspiration.

30

The information in the graph suggests that over time a mouse's brown fat

A) steadily decreases in percentage.

B) steadily decreases in content.

C) notably decreases in percentage and levels off.

D) steadily decreases in content and levels off.

31

Does the information in the graph support the author's statements regarding brown fat percentages in humans?

A) Yes, because its data match exactly the trend the author describes.

B) Yes, because it suggests that all infant mammals have high brown fat levels.

C) No, because it illustrates information contradictory to the author's assertions.

D) No, because it does not provide information relevant to humans.

32

Data in the graph indicate that the greatest percent change in body fat types in mice occurs between

A) 0-10 days.

B) 10-20 days.

C) 20-30 days.

D) 30-40 days.

Questions 33-42 are based on the following passage.

This excerpt is taken from a 1775 speech delivered by Virginia politician Patrick Henry at St. John's Church, Richmond. Designed to incite revolutionary sentiment against Great Britain, Henry's address has since become famous for the rallying cry found in its final lines: "Give me liberty or give me death!"

I have but one lamp by which my feet are guided; and that is the lamp of experience. I know of no way of judging of the future but by the past. And judging by the past, I wish
Line to know what there has been in the conduct of the British
5 ministry for the last ten years, to justify those hopes with which gentlemen have been pleased to solace themselves, and the House? Is it that insidious smile with which our petition has been lately received? Trust it not, sir; it will prove a snare to your feet. Suffer not yourselves to be betrayed with a kiss.
10 Ask yourselves how this gracious reception of our petition comports with these war-like preparations which cover our waters and darken our land. Are fleets and armies necessary to a work of love and reconciliation? Have we shown ourselves so unwilling to be reconciled, that force must be called in to
15 win back our love? Let us not deceive ourselves, sir. These are the implements of war and subjugation; the last arguments to which kings resort. I ask, gentlemen, sir, what means this martial array, if its purpose be not to force us to submission? Can gentlemen assign any other possible motive for it? Has
20 Great Britain any enemy, in this quarter of the world, to call for all this accumulation of navies and armies? No, sir, she has none. They are meant for us; they can be meant for no other. They are sent over to bind and rivet upon us those chains which the British ministry have been so long forging. And what have
25 we to oppose to them? Shall we try argument? Sir, we have been trying that for the last ten years. Have we anything new to offer upon the subject? Nothing.
We have held the subject up in every light of which it is capable, but it has been all in vain. Shall we resort to entreaty
30 and humble supplication? What terms shall we find which have not been already exhausted? Let us not, I beseech you, sir, deceive ourselves. Sir, we have done everything that could be done, to avert the storm which is now coming on. We have petitioned; we have remonstrated; we have supplicated;
35 we have prostrated ourselves before the throne, and have implored its interposition to arrest the tyrannical hands of the ministry and Parliament. Our petitions have been slighted; our remonstrances have produced additional violence and insult; our supplications have been disregarded; and we have
40 been spurned, with contempt, from the foot of the throne. In vain, after these things, may we indulge the fond hope of peace and reconciliation. There is no longer any room for hope. If we wish to be free, if we mean to preserve inviolate

CONTINUE

those inestimable privileges for which we have been so long
45 contending, if we mean not basely to abandon the noble
struggle in which we have been so long engaged, and which
we have pledged ourselves never to abandon until the glorious
object of our contest shall be obtained, we must fight! I repeat
it, sir, we must fight! An appeal to arms and to the God of
50 Hosts is all that is left us!
    They tell us, sir, that we are weak, unable to cope with so
formidable an adversary. But when shall we be stronger? Will
it be the next week, or the next year? Will it be when we are
totally disarmed, and when a British guard shall be stationed
55 in every house? Shall we gather strength by irresolution and
inaction? Shall we acquire the means of effectual resistance,
by lying supinely on our backs, and hugging the delusive
phantom of hope, until our enemies shall have bound us hand
and foot? Sir, we are not weak if we make a proper use of
60 those means which the God of nature hath placed in our power.
Three millions of people, armed in the holy cause of liberty,
and in such a country as that which we possess, are invincible
by any force which our enemy can send against us. Besides,
sir, we shall not fight our battles alone. There is a just God who
65 presides over the destinies of nations, and who will raise up
friends to fight our battles for us. The battle, sir, is not to the
strong alone; it is to the vigilant, the active, the brave.

33

The stance that Henry takes in the passage is best
described as that of

A) an idealist urging a course of action.
B) a scholar explaining a controversy.
C) an observer striving for neutrality.
D) a politician seeking a moderate position.

34

Henry's discussion in lines 10-24 ("Ask yourselves . . .
long forging") indicates that

A) Great Britain will soon begin an armed offensive
against nations all over the world.
B) American rebels are organizing themselves to prepare
for revolution.
C) Great Britain anticipates war against those living in
America.
D) the economic privileges granted to the colonists are
rapidly being revoked.

35

As used in line 19, "assign" most nearly means
A) specify.
B) charge.
C) allocate.
D) authorize.

36

Henry characterizes going to war with Britain as
A) a sure route to defeat.
B) a preventable disaster.
C) a premature decision.
D) a last resort.

37

Which choice provides the best evidence for the answer to
the previous question?
A) Lines 13-15 ("Have we . . . our love?")
B) Lines 29-30 ("Shall we . . . supplication?")
C) Lines 49-50 ("An appeal to . . . left us!")
D) Lines 61-63 ("Three millions . . . against us")

CONTINUE

38

As used in line 36, "arrest" most nearly means

A) check.
B) catch.
C) detain.
D) secure.

39

What is Henry's main point about attempts at peaceful reconciliation?

A) They make Great Britain look weak.
B) They have been tried and found wanting.
C) They will likely culminate in compromise.
D) They are successfully preventing violent war.

40

Henry employs which of the following to strengthen his argument?

A) Rhetorical questions
B) Statistical studies
C) Ironic understatement
D) Literary allusions

41

Which choice provides the best evidence for the answer to the previous question?

A) Lines 1-2 ("I have but . . . experience")
B) Lines 15-17 ("These are . . . resort")
C) Lines 32-33 ("Sir, we . . . coming on")
D) Lines 55-59 ("Shall we . . . and foot?")

42

In the last paragraph, what does Henry predict as the outcome of a war with Great Britain?

A) Great Britain will lose because its soldiers do not have the material resources of the American rebels.
B) Great Britain will win because its soldiers outnumber the American rebels by a significant margin.
C) Great Britain will lose because it is fighting for an unjust cause.
D) Great Britain will win because it has already established footholds in American territory.

CONTINUE

Questions 43-52 are based on the following passage and supplementary material.

This text is adapted from the scientific paper "The Rise of Humanity and the Fall of Megafauna."

New scientific evidence that is coming to light blames humans for the extinction of large animals ("megafauna"), pointing to potentially disastrous consequences for today's global ecosystems. Large land animals were once widely spread over the entire Earth, inhabiting every continent but Antarctica. Many possible explanations have been proposed by scientists to account for the mass extinction of these massive organisms, including climate change, disease, and even the impact of an asteroid or comet. The debate has come down to two prime theories: natural climate change and human hunting.

The term "megafauna" is applicable to any animal weighing more than 100 pounds. Prehistoric megafauna included woolly mammoths, mastodons, cave lions, and giant sloths. All four of these species (and many more) disappeared during what is called the Quaternary Extinction, a global die-off that took place about 12,000 years ago, during the end of the Pleistocene epoch.

As the Pleistocene epoch drew to a close, the Earth went through a period of warming, an episode of climate change on a grand scale. Glaciers retreated, and the "ice age" came to an end. Earlier scientific theories posited that this warming might have been what killed the megafauna. Indeed, as environmental activism picked up steam, the die-off of large terrestrial animals was often used as a warning, a cautionary tale for what could happen in the event of human-driven climate change. Yet the latest research attributes responsibility to a different human factor: overhunting.

A paper published in 2014 in Proceedings of the Royal Society (series B) found strong evidence that human predators caused the extinction of large animals, which were already under stress in a changing environment. Taking a global, statistical analysis of extinction events during the Quaternary Extinction, the paper posited that the arrival of humans was most directly correlated with extinction; climate change was an outside factor. "The evidence really strongly suggests that people were the defining factor," said the leader of the study, Chris Sandom, who conducted the work as a post-doctoral researcher at Denmark's Aarhus University.

Further studies in 2015 added weight to this hypothesis. One study published in 2015 in *Ecography* Magazine considered detailed climate data and compared these figures with information about human movements and hunting patterns. The authors found that "human colonization was the dominant driver of megafaunal extinction across the world but that climatic factors were also important." Many megafauna species were under duress in their changing climate, struggling to adapt to the quickly changing conditions. That meant easy prey for the ascendant hunters, humans.

These studies of prehistoric times have some very contemporary implications. Many modern species fall under the definition "megafauna," including tigers, elephants, and rhinos. Many such megafauna species are threatened by extinction today. Even by the most conservative estimates, "the average rate of vertebrate species loss over the last century is up to 100 times higher than the background rate," according to a recent article in *Science Advances*. And the old dangers have accelerated, too, as new threats arise in the forms of human-caused loss of habitat and human-caused climate change. If we humans aren't careful, we may combine all the largest threats to megafauna into a single, new mass extinction.

Average Loss of Species in 2015

Invertebrates	6%
Vertebrates	12%
Background Rate	.1%

43

The author most likely considers "climate change, disease, and even the impact of an asteroid or comet" (lines 8-9) to be

A) the most important factors contributing to the mass extinction of the megafauna.

B) verified and transformative events occurring within the time period of the Quaternary Extinction.

C) irrelevant considering the damage to megafauna caused by ancient humans.

D) influential but ultimately secondary elements of the Quaternary Extinction.

 CONTINUE

44

As used in line 10, "prime" most nearly means

A) main.

B) early.

C) typical.

D) superior.

45

As used in line 20, "grand" most nearly means

A) extravagant.

B) impressive.

C) widespread.

D) renowned.

46

The research cited in the passage indicates that

A) global warming and natural disasters forced ancient megafauna to move into new habitats.

B) modern megafauna species have largely resisted domestication.

C) changing temperatures killed off the many megafauna that could not adapt to new food sources.

D) the declining population of megafauna was most directly caused by the arrival of ancient humans.

47

Which choice provides the best evidence for the answer to the previous question?

A) Lines 18-20 ("As the . . . scale")

B) Lines 33-35 ("the paper . . . factor")

C) Line 39 ("Further studies . . . hypothesis")

D) Lines 50-52 ("Many modern . . . rhinos")

48

The author of the passage would most likely agree with which of the following statements?

A) Animals considered megafauna today are at substantial risk of extinction due to habitat invasion.

B) Research on the impact of humans on megafauna has resulted in initiatives to preserve the environment.

C) Because of the development of civilization and technology, there are now more factors contributing to the extinction of megafauna than in the past.

D) Contemporary versions of megafauna have evolved to be less vulnerable to mass extinction than their ancient counterparts.

CONTINUE

49

The passage suggests that ancient humans

A) destroyed megafauna habitats that have proven impossible to restore despite the efforts of modern ecologists.

B) were at an advantage over megafauna that had already been weakened by changes in environment and climate.

C) had more highly developed motor skills than modern humans and therefore were able to hunt down and kill many megafauna.

D) exerted a negative influence on megafauna environments through the development of settlements and agriculture.

50

Which choice provides the best evidence for the answer to the previous question?

A) Lines 6-9 ("Many . . . comet")

B) Lines 28-30 ("A paper . . . animals")

C) Lines 45-48 ("Many . . . humans")

D) Lines 56-58 ("And the . . . change")

51

Do the data in the chart support the idea that megafauna today are vulnerable to extinction?

A) Yes, because both the passage and the chart list a vertebrate species loss of over 100 times the background rate.

B) Yes, because the species loss in 2015 is comparable to the species loss during the Quaternary Extinction.

C) No, because the species loss in the chart is higher than the species loss cited in the passage.

D) No, because the chart records the species loss for all vertebrates instead of for megafauna alone.

52

The data in the figure suggest that the extinction rate for invertebrates is

A) increasing more slowly than both the extinction rate for vertebrates and the background rate.

B) directly proportional to the extinction rate for vertebrates and inversely proportional to the background rate.

C) double the extinction rate for vertebrates and significantly higher than the background rate.

D) half the extinction rate for vertebrates and significantly higher than the background rate.

STOP

If you finish before time is called, you may check your work on this section only.

Do not turn to any other section.

No Test Material On This Page

Answer Key: TEST 3

Test 3

PASSAGE 1
Fiction

1.   C
2.   A
3.   B
4.   A
5.   D
6.   B
7.   C
8.   B
9.   A
10. C

PASSAGE 2
Social Science

11. B
12. C
13. A
14. D
15. B
16. D
17. D
18. B
19. A
20. C
21. A

PASSAGE 3
Natural Science 1

22. A
23. B
24. A
25. B
26. C
27. D
28. C
29. B
30. C
31. D
32. A

PASSAGE 4
Global Conversation

33. A
34. C
35. A
36. D
37. C
38. A
39. B
40. A
41. D
42. C

PASSAGE 5
Natural Science 2

43. D
44. A
45. C
46. D
47. B
48. A
49. B
50. C
51. D
52. D

Once you have determined how many questions
you answered correctly, consult the chart on Page 174
to determine your **SAT Reading Test score.**

Please visit **ies2400.com/answers** for answer explanations.

Post-Test Analysis

This post-test analysis is essential if you want to see an improvement on your next test. Possible reasons for errors on the five passages in this test are listed here. Place check marks next to the types of errors that pertain to you, or write your own types of errors in the blank spaces.

TIMING AND ACCURACY

◇   Spent too long reading individual passages
◇   Spent too long answering each question
◇   Spent too long on a few difficult questions
◇   Felt rushed and made silly mistakes or random errors
◇   Unable to work quickly using textual evidence and POE

Other: _____

APPROACHING THE PASSAGES AND QUESTIONS

◇   Unable to effectively grasp a passage's tone or style
◇   Unable to effectively grasp a passage's topic or stance
◇   Did not understand the context of line references
◇   Did not eliminate false answers using strong evidence
◇   Answered questions using first impressions instead of POE
◇   Answered questions without checking or inserting final answer
◇   Eliminated correct answer during POE
◇   Consistent trouble with Word in Context vocabulary
◇   Consistent trouble with Command of Evidence questions
◇   Consistent trouble with passage comparison questions

Other: _____

> **Use this form** to better analyze your performance. If you don't understand why you made errors, there is no way that you can correct them!

FICTION: # CORRECT_____   # WRONG _____   # OMITTED _____

◇   Could not grasp the roles and attitudes of major characters
◇   Could not grasp the significance of particular scenes or images
◇   Difficulty understanding the author's style and language
◇   Difficulty understanding the tone, theme, and structure of the passage as a whole

Other: _____

SOCIAL SCIENCE AND
GLOBAL CONVERSATION: # CORRECT_____   # WRONG _____   # OMITTED _____

◇   Unable to grasp the overall argument or thesis of an individual passage
◇   Unable to work effectively with the specific data or evidence in a passage
◇   Unable to respond effectively to tone, structure, and vocabulary
◇   Difficulty working with the graphics and graphic questions in a Social Science passage
◇   Difficulty understanding the logic or methodology of a Social Science passage
◇   Difficulty with the style and language of a Global Conversation passage
◇   Difficulty with the main historical and political concepts of a Global Conversation passage

Other: _____

NATURAL SCIENCE: # CORRECT_____   # WRONG _____   # OMITTED _____

◇   Unable to grasp the overall argument or thesis of an individual passage
◇   Unable to work effectively with the specific data or evidence in a passage
◇   Unable to respond effectively to tone, structure, and vocabulary
◇   Difficulty understanding the significance of the theories or experiments presented
◇   Difficulty working with the graphics and graphic questions

Other: _____

TEST 4

Test 4

Reading Test
65 MINUTES, 52 QUESTIONS

Turn to Section 1 of your answer sheet to answer the questions in this section.

Questions 1-10 are based on the following passage.

The passage that follows is taken from a collection of related short stories. In the episode provided below, Gregory, a man of about thirty years-old, takes a brief vacation in order to escape his day-to-day worries.

It had not been, Gregory decided, the most intelligent decision he had ever made. While it had seemed like a good idea at the time, he was certainly not laughing now.
Line He had reached the small hotel the previous night. Though
5 weighed down and exhausted when he had arrived, he had arisen the next morning to the fresh, rejuvenating light flooding though the little window. He had leapt out of bed, showered, dressed, and eaten breakfast with an invigoration he had not felt in years.
10 During his morning walk, he had found the little path beside the creek that trickled down the hill. The hill had not been too difficult to mount, and it was not long before Gregory reached the higher elevation of the moors. In every direction, the purple-tinted heather stretched away, seemingly limitless,
15 until it touched the soaring sky of the horizon. For the first time in months, he felt free and confident. It was as though with each step of the climb he shed one more of the arguments, the worries, the demands, the moments of lonely poverty that his life had accumulated over the years. He gazed around
20 delightedly, then he flung his arms out as far as he could and ran forward, feeling the laughter bubbling up inside him, feeling transformed into a child again, dashing free.
Eventually, he stopped and leaned against one of the rocks, panting and giggling. He stared up at the clear light. When
25 was the last time he had felt like this? Perhaps it had been that moment when, finally released from work and family, he had set foot in rural India and embraced the welcoming warmth

of that ancient earth for the first time. Everything had seemed possible then, just as it did now.
30 All day, he wandered carelessly on the moors, not really bothering about direction. He watched lizards dart across the rocks. He rolled in the heather and lay on his back, regarding the butterflies that skittered around him and the birds that sailed on the currents of air high above. He closed his eyes and listened to
35 the subtle vibrations of the land and the distant barking of dogs.
It was rain that woke him. The sky had darkened and the wind had grown frigid. He pulled his jacket closer to his body and looked around. The moor seemed different now in the dusk, almost treacherous in its vast uniformity. He stood up stiffly
40 and set off in what he thought was the right direction. The rain intensified. His feet and hands were numb. He stopped and peered around. He had no idea where he was. He found shelter under an overhanging rock face and pondered what to do; he could not simply stay here on the moor and hope to be rescued.
45 Here he was, alone and out of reach, blundering through this dark and empty vastness.
He set out. How long he traveled though the darkness, he did not know. To begin with, he felt only the lash of rain and wind against his sodden body; eventually, he just accepted his
50 discomfort and found ways to put his outward afflictions out of mind. He held imaginary conversations with all those people he had deserted in the past, reasoning with them, patiently informing them that what he had done had been justified. Each attempt at explanation petered out: his attempts always had.
55 He felt only his own exhaustion and then, quite unexpectedly, he found himself falling. His head came into contact with something hard and he lost consciousness.
He awoke to find a hot tongue persistently but gently licking his face. For a moment he submitted, then stirred himself. A
60 blazing light dazzled him and he promptly shut his eyes. He heard a voice.

CONTINUE

"You're not dead, then? I thought you were at first. Nasty fall, that; lots of deadly patches in these parts. You're lucky the dog found you. Come on. It's time to come out of the
65 darkness and join the land of the living again."

Gregory thought about this for a moment, the land of the living, and then relaxed. Perhaps it was time.

1

At the beginning of Gregory's walk, Gregory's attitude is best described as

A) pragmatic.

B) cheerful.

C) ashamed.

D) anxious.

2

Which choice provides the best evidence for the answer to the previous question?

A) Line 3 ("he was . . . now")

B) Lines 4-7 ("Though weighed . . . window")

C) Lines 15-16 ("For the first . . . confident")

D) Lines 45-46 ("Here he . . . vastness")

3

The statement in lines 16-19 ("It was . . . years") most directly suggests that Gregory

A) was experiencing an increased sense of well-being.

B) had overcome unusually difficult circumstances.

C) was coping with his problems in a responsible manner.

D) ordinarily avoided stressful situations in his life.

4

As used in line 32, "regarding" most nearly means

A) reconsidering.

B) judging.

C) describing.

D) watching.

5

The effect of lines 36-39 ("It was . . . uniformity") is to suggest that Gregory's surroundings had become

A) disorienting yet emboldening.

B) restricted and uncomfortable.

C) unfamiliar and potentially hazardous.

D) cold and wet but still navigable.

6

It can be reasonably inferred that Gregory held "imaginary conversations" (line 51) in order to

A) better understand his new surroundings.

B) distract himself from his present suffering.

C) alleviate his guilt about past decisions.

D) justify his unusual life choices.

7

Which choice provides the best evidence for the answer to the previous question?

A) Lines 1-2 ("It had not . . . ever made")

B) Lines 47-48 ("How long . . . not know")

C) Lines 48-51 ("To begin . . . mind")

D) Lines 53-54 ("Each attempt . . . always had")

CONTINUE 65

8

As used in line 50, "outward" most nearly means

A) notable.

B) physical.

C) superficial.

D) expansive.

9

Gregory's reaction to the comments in lines 62-65 most strongly suggests that he felt a sense of

A) nervous anticipation.

B) grudging acceptance.

C) eager compliance.

D) relieved resignation.

10

As a whole, the passage can best be described as an account of

A) a serious conflict punctuated by moments of comedy.

B) a man's ambitious travels through an alien and lifeless setting.

C) a journey that leads to moments of self-reflection.

D) an individual's attainment of a more sophisticated world view.

Questions 11-21 are based on the following passage and supplementary material.

This reading is adapted from the essay "The Rise of Robotics: Is Unskilled Labor the First Domino to Fall?" by Nathaniel Hunt.

With new developments in robotics and artificial intelligence, technological advancement is rapidly transforming from a benevolent force to one that frightens many Americans.
Line Commentators have predicted since the 1960s that unskilled
5   labor would eventually be replaced by machinery, but it's only now that the vision is becoming a reality.
Recently, offshore manufacturing has been coming back to the US—but because of automation, this trend is creating fewer jobs than had been hoped. Lured by tax breaks, workers
10 desperate for any kind of work, and cotton subsidies, at least 20 Chinese firms have decided to open new textile factories in North and South Carolina. Each factory is highly automated, relying on machines and robots to do the work that thousands of humans once performed. In one planned factory, for
15 example, the Keer Group is expecting to hire only 500 workers to supplement its automated assembly line.
Restaurant and fast food workers are already feeling the sting of robotics. The Huffington Post went so far as to call the phenomenon an imminent "Robot Armageddon," pointing
20 to new advances in technology that could threaten to replace cooks and cashiers. For instance, a new company named Momentum Machines has created a robot that can crank out 360 burgers per hour. Academic research reinforces the possibility of burgeoning robot labor: in 2014, researchers at
25 Oxford University declared that there is a 92% chance that the fast-food industry will become widely automated in the next decade or two.
The question must be raised: is this automation good for globalized civilizations? In a global market that still relies
30 so much on unskilled labor, what happens when robots and machines become so sophisticated that they make human employees obsolete?
Even semi-skilled jobs are disappearing. One company widely praised for its realignment of existing business, Uber,
35 is relentlessly advancing toward automating its vehicles. Though this car-hire service routinely points to how many jobs it's created or intends to create in the world economy (a goal of 50,000 new jobs in Europe in 2015, for example), the corporate leadership makes no secret of Uber's push for new
40 technologies. Uber CEO Travis Kalanick has been open about his plans to eliminate every single one of the jobs his company has provided: "The reason Uber could be expensive is you're paying for the other dude in the car. When there is no other dude in the car, the cost of taking an Uber anywhere is cheaper.
45 Even on a road trip."

 CONTINUE

Even more frightening is the thought that skilled occupations are next. As entrepreneur and author Vivek Wadhwa explains, "Within 10 years . . . artificial intelligence-based systems will start doing the jobs of most office workers
50 in accounting, finance, and administration." He warns that the same phenomenon will affect pharmacists, paralegals, customer-support staff, and other skilled professions. Even doctors may soon be replaced by biometric sensors and AI. And he is not alone in emphasizing the problems of
55 automatized labor. Jerry Kaplan of Stanford University believes that income inequality and unemployment are two of the biggest problems of the 21st century—and that "a major cause of both of those is the accelerating progress of technology in general, and of artificial intelligence in
60 particular."

Other commentators are more optimistic, however. Steve Denning, a writer at *Forbes*, thinks that as robots replace labor, more humans will move into service jobs. In the service sector, human beings can provide rich interpersonal experience, which
65 is a valuable commodity in the age of sterile and disillusioning machine interaction. Even Wadhwa himself sees potential for job growth in tourism and recreation, and dreams of a possible utopian future: "What if we could be working 10 or 15 hours per week from anywhere we want and have the remaining
70 time for leisure, social work, or attainment of knowledge?" If human society can restructure itself as dramatically as that, we might be able to usher in a technological paradise. Yet based on humanity's track record when it comes to restructuring, it will be a bumpy ride—if we get there at all.

11

According to the passage, which choice best describes the author's answer to the question raised in lines 28-29?

A) Society will probably face great obstacles in adapting to new technologies.

B) People will succeed in integrating artificial intelligence into everyday life.

C) Civilizations will become completely unrecognizable in the next decade.

D) It is certain that automation will only have positive consequences.

12

Which choice provides the best evidence for the answer to the previous question?

A) Lines 2-3 ("technological . . . Americans")

B) Lines 38-40 ("the corporate . . . technologies")

C) Lines 61-63 ("Steve . . . jobs")

D) Lines 72-74 ("Yet based . . . at all")

13

As used in line 19, "imminent" most nearly means

A) impending.

B) important.

C) recent.

D) predictable.

Human and Automated Workers in U.S. Factories

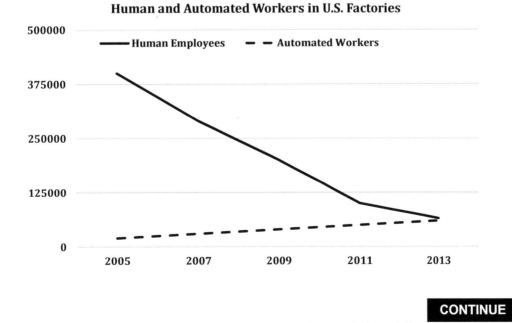

— Human Employees   – – Automated Workers

14

According to the passage, those who oppose automated labor believe that

A) offshore manufacturing will ensure the survival of human labor.

B) the automation of unskilled labor does not foretell the automation of skilled labor.

C) social disparity is a direct result of increasingly advanced technology.

D) the average person will only have 10 or 15 hours of work a week.

15

Which choice provides the best evidence for the answer to the previous question?

A) Lines 12-14 ("Each . . . performed")

B) Lines 42-43 ("The reason . . . car")

C) Lines 57-60 ("a major . . . in general")

D) Lines 64-66 ("human . . . interaction")

16

The author uses the word "only" in line 15 primarily to suggest that

A) too few people will be hired to efficiently run the factory.

B) there is not enough skilled labor to fill all the vacancies.

C) the Keer Group will hire more people than it anticipated.

D) the company can hire fewer people because of automation.

17

The primary purpose of the statistic in line 25 is to

A) create doubt about the inevitability of an automated future.

B) indicate the aptness of a viewpoint discussed in the paragraph.

C) suggest that only unskilled labor will be replaced by robots.

D) illustrate that robot labor is more efficient.

18

It can most reasonably be inferred that Vivek Wadhwa believes that

A) fear of automation is completely unwarranted.

B) artificial intelligence has the potential to be both harmful and helpful.

C) society will not evolve to accommodate new technologies.

D) there is no reason to hope that improvement will result from automation.

19

As used in line 32, "obsolete" most nearly means

A) fossilized.

B) old-fashioned.

C) irrelevant.

D) absurd.

20

The author of the passage would most likely react to the data in the graph with

A) enthusiasm, because the graph indicates that humans will have shorter working hours and more time for recreation and leisure.

B) alarm, because increased human dependence on robots and machines will hinder scientific and technological progress.

C) concern, because the loss of unskilled labor jobs to machines could endanger semi-skilled and skilled occupations.

D) nonchalance, because humans will learn to adapt and create new jobs that cannot be performed by automation alone.

21

It can be inferred from the data in the chart that

A) The number of human employees decreased at a steady rate between 2005 and 2013.

B) The number of automated workers increased at a steady rate between 2005 and 2013.

C) The number of human workers will remain roughly the same from 2013 on.

D) The number of automated workers will be significantly greater than the number of human workers from 2013 on.

CONTINUE

Questions 22-31 are based on the following passages.

In 2006, a new dispute in astronomy arose when Pluto, long regarded as the ninth planet in our solar system, was downgraded from "planet" to "dwarf planet." Below, two authors look back and consider the events and opinions surrounding Pluto's re-classification.

Passage 1

International astronomy organizations were thrown into controversy in 2005, when a new solar object was discovered. This stellar body, called "Eris," is farther from the sun than
Line any other major heavenly body in our solar system. Though
5 it's three times as far from the sun as Pluto is, Eris is also 27% more massive than Pluto. This new discovery, and the resulting questions (should Eris be classified as a planet?) shook the International Astronomical Union (IAU), leading this organization to formally define the term "planet" for the
10 first time. The largest 8 planets were untouched, but Pluto was demoted from "planet" to "dwarf planet." However, according to many astronomers, including NASA scientists, Pluto should be returned to its original status.

Scientists have pointed out that there are a number of
15 problems with the definition adopted by the IAU. By current criteria, the astronomical objects outside our own solar system cannot be classified as planets—a problem when "90 per cent of the planets we know now are outside our solar system," according to Dr. David Morrison, the director of NASA's Lunar
20 Science Institute.

Alan Sterns, the principal investigator for the New Horizons Pluto mission, scoffs at the IAU's attempts to demote Pluto. He maintains that Pluto is in fact a planet, with many planetary attributes: a core, geology, seasons, an atmosphere,
25 clouds, several moons, and maybe even a polar ice cap. Responding to the use of size as the main attribute that the IAU uses to classify planets, Dr. Sterns jokes that dwelling on planetary size is akin to saying that one breed of animal is a different species if it's smaller than other yet otherwise similar
30 breeds. "I like to say, a Chihuahua is still a dog," he says.

Sterns further claims that simple human expediency is driving the push to keep Pluto non-planetary. "Some scientists said, well, that's too many planets. I don't think I can remember all of the names of those, so . . . we have to find
35 some way of limiting the number of planets." Needless to say, Sterns is not shy about submitting those who downgraded Pluto to a little degradation.

Passage 2

There has been much fuss lately in both the scientific and lay communities regarding the fact that Pluto is no longer
40 considered a planet. The International Astronomical Union (IAU) defines a planet as a celestial body that: 1. is in orbit around the Sun, 2. has sufficient mass to assume hydrostatic equilibrium (a nearly round shape), and 3. has "cleared the neighborhood" around its orbit. The first two parts of the IAU
45 definition are fairly straightforward: Pluto certainly orbits our Sun and is nearly round. The third prong of the definition is the one responsible for Pluto's demotion from planet to dwarf planet. Pluto has not "cleared the neighborhood" around its orbit of other celestial bodies. Pluto's orbit intersects Neptune's
50 and so, in addition to being a dwarf planet, Pluto is also classified as a Trans-Neptunian Object (TNO).

There are more than 1,000 TNOs now known to scientists, one of which, Eris, has its own moon. Even before the final NASA calculations were in (Eris is slightly larger and
55 approximately 27% more massive than Pluto), scientists were sure that Eris was the ninth most massive object orbiting our Sun. "It's definitely bigger than Pluto," commented Mike Brown, a professor of planetary astronomy. Eris, like Pluto, has not "cleared the neighborhood" and is thus not a planet.

60 Some scientists, such as Dr. David Morrison, have argued that the IAU definition of a planet is preposterously narrow because it requires that a planet orbit not just any star in the universe but specifically our star, the Sun. That, it is argued, excludes the vast majority of planets from the IAU
65 definition. However, Dr. Morrison and his cohorts fail to address the fact that the IAU acknowledges the category of "exoplanets" (planets outside of our solar system). Thus, Dr. Morrison skirts the issue of whether Pluto has (exo)planetary characteristics. Pluto is certainly not an exoplanet because it
70 isn't outside of our solar system, and so the issue of whether it should be classified as a planet revolves around its "uncleared neighborhood."

22

The primary purpose of Passage 1 is to

A) highlight the accomplishments of Dr. Morrison and Dr. Sterns.

B) shed light on the discovery of a new stellar body.

C) catalogue Pluto's planetary attributes.

D) critique the recent reclassification of Pluto.

23

As used in line 21, "principal" most nearly means

A) fundamental.

B) chief.

C) superior.

D) most liable.

24

According to the experts cited in Passage 1, the IAU classification of planets

A) should not depend solely on size.

B) requires the presence of a central star.

C) designates Pluto as an exoplanet.

D) settles the controversy over Pluto's status.

25

According to the author of Passage 2, Dr. Morrison is guilty of

A) holding to a narrow definition of planets.

B) agreeing with the IAU classifications.

C) believing that planets need to orbit the Sun.

D) ignoring the idea of exoplanets.

26

It can most reasonably be inferred that the author of Passage 1 and the author of Passage 2 would both agree that Eris is

A) irrefutably more massive than Pluto.

B) deserving of planetary status.

C) a reasonable justification for Pluto's demotion.

D) the source of controversy in astronomy.

27

According to Passage 1, the non-planetary status of Pluto

A) reflects the definition of a planet shared by all astronomers.

B) could stem from scientists' desire to simplify the study of planets.

C) cannot be disputed by non-scientists.

D) is deserved since Pluto lacks all planetary characteristics.

28

Which choice provides the best evidence for the answer to the previous question?

A) Lines 1-2 ("International . . . discovered")

B) Lines 11-13 ("However . . . status")

C) Lines 21-23 ("Alan . . . Pluto")

D) Lines 32-35 ("Some . . . planets")

29

It can most reasonably be inferred that the author of Passage 2 would respond to the idea presented in lines 26-27 ("the use . . . planets") by stating that

A) planetary size is the main reason Pluto is not a planet.

B) Pluto is an exoplanet, not a dwarf planet.

C) Dr. Sterns has a comprehensive understanding of astronomy.

D) the IAU uses a different criterion to disqualify Pluto.

30

Which choice provides the best evidence for the answer to the previous question?

A) Lines 38-40 ("There . . . planet")

B) Lines 46-48 ("The third . . . planet")

C) Lines 50-51 ("Pluto . . . Object")

D) Lines 55-57 ("scientists . . . Sun")

31

As used in line 49, "intersects" most nearly means

A) crosses.

B) bisects.

C) disrupts.

D) separates.

CONTINUE

Questions 32-41 are based on the following passage.

This passage is taken from *Crime: Its Cause and Treatment*, a book by the celebrated American attorney Clarence Darrow (1857-1938).

Those who have had no experience in the courts and no knowledge of what is known as the "criminal class" have a general idea that a criminal is not like other men. The people
Line they know are law-abiding, conventional believers in the
5 State and the Church and all social customs and relations; they have strict ideas of property rights, and regard the law as sacred. True, they have no more acquaintance with law-makers and politicians in general than with the criminal class, which, of course, is one reason why they have such unbounded
10 confidence in the law. Such persons are surprised and shocked when some member of the family or some friend is entangled in the courts, and generally regard it as a catastrophe that has come upon him by accident or a terrible mistake. As a rule, they do all in their power to help him whether he is acquitted
15 or convicted. They never think that he and everyone else they know is not materially different from the ordinary criminal. As a matter of fact, the potential criminal is in every man, and no one was ever so abandoned that some friend would not plead for him, or that some one who knew him would not testify to
20 his good deeds.
The criminal is not hard to understand. He is one who, from inherited defects or from great misfortune or especially hard circumstances, is not able to make the necessary adjustments to fit him to his environment. Seldom is he a man
25 of average intelligence, unless he belongs to a certain class that will be discussed later. Almost always he is below the normal of intelligence and in perhaps half of the cases very much below. Nearly always he is a person of practically no education and no property. One who has given attention to the subject of
30 crime knows exactly where the criminal comes from and how he will develop. The crimes of violence and murder, and the lesser crimes against property, practically all come from those who have been reared in the poor and congested districts of cities and large villages. The robbers, burglars, pickpockets and
35 thieves are from these surroundings. In a broad sense, some criminals are born and some are made. Nearly all of them are both born and made. This does not mean that criminality can be inherited, or even that there is a criminal type. It means that with certain physical and mental imperfections and with certain
40 environment the criminal will be the result.
Seldom does one begin a criminal life as a full-grown man. The origin of the typical criminal is an imperfect child, suffering from some defect. Usually he was born with a weak intellect, or an unstable nervous system. He comes from poor
45 parents. Often one or both of these died or met misfortune while he was young. He comes from the crowded part of a poor district. He has had little chance to go to school and could not have been a scholar, no matter how regularly he attended school. Some useful things he could have learned had society
50 furnished the right teachers, surroundings, and opportunities to make the most of an imperfect child.

32

Darrow's primary purpose in this passage is to
A) show why crime rates are increasing in crowded cities.
B) urge greater leniency towards all but the worst criminals
C) explain the origins of criminal activity.
D) distinguish different types of criminals.

33

Darrow uses the word "poor" throughout the passage mainly to
A) imply that an underprivileged upbringing leads to disrespect for the property of others.
B) indicate that social and economic reforms will make crime much less common.
C) symbolize the moral state of many of those who grow up to commit crimes.
D) emphasize the lifestyle of deprivation that is faced by many who become criminals.

34

As used in line 9, "unbounded" most nearly means
A) liberated.
B) enlightened.
C) thorough.
D) expressive.

35

Darrow mentions "acquaintance with law-makers and politicians" (lines 7-8) in order to
A) encourage greater respect for authority.
B) discuss the paradoxical nature of individualism.
C) underscore the need for reform.
D) explain the origins of a viewpoint.

36

In this passage, Darrow argues against the assumption that

A) all criminals are guided by hereditary factors.

B) good education could prevent criminal activity.

C) most Americans are uninterested in the legal system.

D) highly intelligent people will show compassion for criminals.

37

Which choice provides the best evidence for the answer to the previous question?

A) Lines 1-3 ("Those who . . . other men")

B) Lines 26-28 ("Almost always . . . much below")

C) Lines 36-38 ("Nearly all . . . criminal type")

D) Lines 49-51 ("Some useful . . . child")

38

As used in line 50, "furnished" most nearly means

A) enhanced.

B) equipped.

C) supplied.

D) nominated.

39

According to Darrow, the acquaintances of criminals tend to view criminals with

A) indifference.

B) bewilderment.

C) fear.

D) sympathy.

40

Which choice provides the best evidence for the answer to the previous question?

A) Lines 3-7 ("The people . . . as sacred")

B) Lines 7-10 ("True, they . . . the law")

C) Lines 16-20 ("As a matter . . . good deeds")

D) Lines 29-31 ("One who . . . develop")

41

The "typical criminal" in the final paragraph is best described as

A) insensitive to events that would disturb most people.

B) subject to circumstances beyond his control.

C) desperate to escape a lifestyle marked by struggle.

D) oblivious to the negative judgments of society.

CONTINUE

Test 4

Questions 42-52 are based on the following passage and supplementary material.

In this passage, an ecologist discusses a means of energy production in the contemporary United Kingdom.

Dinorwig is a village in Wales that lies at the foot of a mountain the locals call Elidir Fawr. In such a landscape and surrounded by such names, the visitor might be forgiven for
Line thinking he has stumbled into the setting of a TV fantasy epic.
5 Disappointingly, perhaps, that is not so, although Elidir Fawr does have another name among the villagers: the Electric Mountain. They know that the mountain has nothing to do with pop entertainment and everything to do with the search for efficient energy through hydro-power.
10 Hydro-power, of course, is nothing new. From the invention of the first water-mill, man has used the control of moving water to his advantage. Hydro-electric power simply raises this control to further sophistication. When the great Hoover Dam in Colorado was built during the years of the
15 Great Depression, this structure's purpose was two-fold: to provide irrigation by controlling the wayward manners of the Colorado River and to generate electric power for over one million homes. The Dam ultimately fueled the development of Las Vegas, Phoenix, and Los Angeles. The success of this
20 achievement encouraged other countries to follow suit.
Although power created in this fashion is relatively cheap—after the cost of actually building the dam is absorbed—there are disadvantages to this form of power creation. One drawback is quite basic—clogging. Large
25 reservoirs are inevitably created above large dams, disturbing the historic rate of water flow within the original river or stream and interrupting the previous enrichment of the lowland below the dam. (Left to their own devices, rivers will both carry off rocks and bring fertilizing silt to new grounds.) Furthermore,
30 the debris which, before the construction of a dam, would have been carried ever-forward by the river to the ocean, is deposited in the reservoir until it blocks all flow of water completely. These disruptions to the traditional importance of rivers can have far-reaching effects; it is even believed that climate
35 change can result from such irregularities.
The Electric Mountain avoids many of these problems. Water is stored in the small lake of Marchlyn Mawr in the upper heights of Elidir Fawr. When required, the water is pumped through sixteen kilometers of tunnel inside the
40 mountain itself, until this water reaches the six power-generating units built into the mountain's very heart. Here, the flow of the water is regulated through the turbines and the resulting energy is transformed into electricity, which is transferred to and distributed by the National Grid that passes
45 power throughout the country. The water, its energizing power utilized, is then pumped into Llyn Peris, a man-made lake lower down the mountain. Later, the pumps in the mountain will be placed into reverse, and the water will be pumped back from Llyn Peris and through the mountain to Marchlyn Mawr.
50 This setup is stunning and original, but is it an example of renewable and low-effort energy in the same sense that the Hoover Dam facility is? In truth, Elidir Fawr was never designed for use as a renewable energy power station. Originally, it was designed as an auxiliary structure that would
55 help sustain a nuclear power matrix. From shutdown, the typical nuclear power station takes almost a week to reach the point of full production, leaving an entire area without energy during this power-up. The Electric Mountain was conceived to solve this problem. However, incidents such as Three Mile
60 Island, Fukushima, Chernobyl, and Sellafield (along with science-fiction hysteria) have diminished public appreciation of nuclear power as an answer to today's energy crisis.
With Wales's nuclear ambitions abandoned, the Electric Mountain's revised role is to supply the necessary input at
65 times when there is a sudden surge in the use of electricity—for example, at the end of an episode of a real TV fantasy epic, when viewers rise in unison from their armchairs to switch on their teakettles. At such times, Elidir Fawr is prepared.

Average Annual Electric Power Production

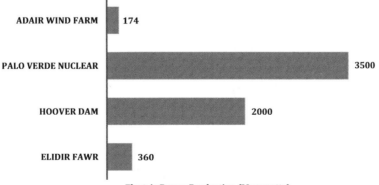

ADAIR WIND FARM 174

PALO VERDE NUCLEAR 3500

HOOVER DAM 2000

ELIDIR FAWR 360

Electric Power Production (Megawatts)

42

The main purpose of the passage is to

A) provide an overview of hydro-power and hydro-electric power and consider the environmental implications of these methods.

B) inform the reader about a particular way of creating energy and describe a successful source of hydro-electric power.

C) propose a new means of energy production and discuss its advantages over the current system of generating electric power.

D) compare and contrast hydro-electric power and nuclear power in order to advocate for the continued use of hydro-electric technology.

43

According to the passage, hydro-electric power

A) is a powerful but dangerous means of harnessing energy and is therefore too risky to implement nationwide.

B) is by no means new technology, and has been used in agriculture and manufacturing for hundreds of years.

C) is a cost-effective and efficient way to create energy but can sometimes have negative effects.

D) is convenient but inherently flawed because of its high cost compared to the amount of energy produced.

44

Which choice provides the best evidence for the answer to the previous question?

A) Lines 10-12 ("Hydro-power . . . advantage")

B) Lines 21-24 ("Although . . . creation")

C) Lines 33-34 ("These disruptions . . . effects")

D) Lines 41-45 ("Here . . . country")

45

As used in line 23, "absorbed" most nearly means

A) soaked up.

B) assimilated.

C) earned back.

D) occupied.

46

The passage indicates that the Electric Mountain

A) successfully avoids the ecological risks normally associated with hydro-electric power.

B) uses technology that is too outdated to be considered a reliable source of hydro-electric energy.

C) is an environmentally friendly and efficient source of electricity and energy on a large scale.

D) uses a less predictable and stable means of harvesting energy than hydro-power or nuclear power.

47

Which choice provides the best evidence for the answer to the previous question?

A) Lines 2-4 ("In such . . . epic")

B) Lines 7-9 ("They know . . . hydro-power")

C) Lines 24-28 ("Large reservoirs . . . the dam")

D) Lines 34-36 ("it is . . . problems")

48

What is the main idea of the fifth paragraph (lines 50-62)?

A) Elidir Fawr was constructed for a much different purpose than other hydro-electric structures such as the Hoover Dam.

B) The Electric Mountain was originally designed as a source of clean, renewable energy that would replace nuclear power stations in the area.

C) Nuclear power sites in Wales are generally safer and less dangerous than other power stations such as Three Mile Island and Chernobyl.

D) Hydro-electric power similar to that created by Elidir Fawr has the capacity to take the place of nuclear energy as a reliable source of electricity.

CONTINUE

Test 4

49

The author indicates that hydro-electric dams are attractive on account of their

A) potential to mitigate global warming.

B) negligible effect on local ecosystems.

C) ability to produce power inexpensively.

D) use of common construction materials.

50

According to the graph, the average electric power production of Elidir Fawr is roughly

A) half of the Adair Wind Farm's.

B) four times the Adair Wind Farm's.

C) half of the Hoover Dam's.

D) one-tenth of Palo Verde Nuclear's.

51

Which concept is supported by the passage and by the information in the graph?

A) The Electric Mountain's level of energy production makes it an ideal power source for a large city.

B) Elidir Fawr is incapable of providing energy on a large scale.

C) The Hoover Dam is more cost efficient than the Adair Wind Farm.

D) Nuclear power plants have been replaced by other means of energy production in recent years.

52

One megawatt can supply energy for almost 1000 people. According to the information in the graph and the passage, a city of 4 million people would most likely have a source of energy similar to

A) Elidir Fawr.

B) the Hoover Dam.

C) the Adair Wind Farm.

D) Palo Verde Nuclear.

STOP

If you finish before time is called, you may check your work on this section only.

Do not turn to any other section.

Answer Key: TEST 4

Test 4

PASSAGE 1
Fiction

1. B
2. C
3. A
4. D
5. C
6. B
7. C
8. B
9. D
10. C

PASSAGE 2
Social Science

11. A
12. D
13. A
14. C
15. C
16. D
17. B
18. B
19. C
20. C
21. B

PASSAGE 3
Natural Science 1

22. D
23. B
24. A
25. D
26. A
27. B
28. D
29. D
30. B
31. A

PASSAGE 4
Global Conversation

32. C
33. D
34. C
35. D
36. A
37. C
38. C
39. D
40. C
41. B

PASSAGE 5
Natural Science 2

42. B
43. C
44. B
45. C
46. A
47. D
48. A
49. C
50. D
51. B
52. D

Once you have determined how many questions
you answered correctly, consult the chart on Page 174
to determine your **SAT Reading Test score.**

Please visit **ies2400.com/answers** for answer explanations.

Post-Test Analysis

This post-test analysis is essential if you want to see an improvement on your next test. Possible reasons for errors on the five passages in this test are listed here. Place check marks next to the types of errors that pertain to you, or write your own types of errors in the blank spaces.

TIMING AND ACCURACY

◇ Spent too long reading individual passages
◇ Spent too long answering each question
◇ Spent too long on a few difficult questions
◇ Felt rushed and made silly mistakes or random errors
◇ Unable to work quickly using textual evidence and POE
Other: _____

APPROACHING THE PASSAGES AND QUESTIONS

◇ Unable to effectively grasp a passage's tone or style
◇ Unable to effectively grasp a passage's topic or stance
◇ Did not understand the context of line references
◇ Did not eliminate false answers using strong evidence
◇ Answered questions using first impressions instead of POE
◇ Answered questions without checking or inserting final answer
◇ Eliminated correct answer during POE
◇ Consistent trouble with Word in Context vocabulary
◇ Consistent trouble with Command of Evidence questions
◇ Consistent trouble with passage comparison questions
Other: _____

> **Use this form** to better analyze your performance. If you don't understand why you made errors, there is no way that you can correct them!

FICTION: # CORRECT_____ # WRONG _____ # OMITTED _____

◇ Could not grasp the roles and attitudes of major characters
◇ Could not grasp the significance of particular scenes or images
◇ Difficulty understanding the author's style and language
◇ Difficulty understanding the tone, theme, and structure of the passage as a whole
Other: _____

SOCIAL SCIENCE AND
GLOBAL CONVERSATION: # CORRECT_____ # WRONG _____ # OMITTED _____

◇ Unable to grasp the overall argument or thesis of an individual passage
◇ Unable to work effectively with the specific data or evidence in a passage
◇ Unable to respond effectively to tone, structure, and vocabulary
◇ Difficulty working with the graphics and graphic questions in a Social Science passage
◇ Difficulty understanding the logic or methodology of a Social Science passage
◇ Difficulty with the style and language of a Global Conversation passage
◇ Difficulty with the main historical and political concepts of a Global Conversation passage
Other: _____

NATURAL SCIENCE: # CORRECT_____ # WRONG _____ # OMITTED _____

◇ Unable to grasp the overall argument or thesis of an individual passage
◇ Unable to work effectively with the specific data or evidence in a passage
◇ Unable to respond effectively to tone, structure, and vocabulary
◇ Difficulty understanding the significance of the theories or experiments presented
◇ Difficulty working with the graphics and graphic questions
Other: _____

TEST 5

Test 5

Reading Test
65 MINUTES, 52 QUESTIONS

Turn to Section 1 of your answer sheet to answer the questions in this section.

DIRECTIONS

Each passage or pair of passages below is followed by a number of questions. After reading each passage or pair, choose the best answer to each question based on what is stated or implied in the passage or passages and in any accompanying graphics (such as a table or graph).

Questions 1-10 are based on the following passage.

This passage is from Charles Dickens, *Dombey and Son*, originally published in 1848. In the following episode, Dickens describes a widowed businessman, Mr. Dombey, and his young son Paul.

Little Paul and his father were the strangest pair at such a time that ever firelight shone upon. Mr. Dombey so erect and solemn, gazing at the blare; Paul's little image, with an old,
Line old face, peering into the red perspective with the fixed and
5 rapt attention of a sage. Mr. Dombey entertaining complicated worldly schemes and plans; the little image entertaining Heaven knows what wild fancies, half-formed thoughts, and wandering speculations; Mr. Dombey stiff with starch and arrogance; the little image by inheritance, and in unconscious imitation. The
10 two so very much alike, and yet so monstrously contrasted.

On one of these occasions, when they had both been perfectly quiet for a long time, and Mr. Dombey only knew that the child was awake by occasionally glancing at his eye, where the bright fire was sparkling like a jewel, little Paul broke
15 silence thus:

"Papa! what's money?"

The abrupt question had such immediate reference to the subject of Mr. Dombey's thoughts, that Mr. Dombey was quite disconcerted.

20 "What is money, Paul?" he answered. "Money?"

"Yes," said the child, laying his hands upon the elbows of his little chair, and turning the old face up towards Mr. Dombey's; "what is money?"

Mr. Dombey was in a difficulty. He would have liked to
25 give him some explanation involving the terms circulating-medium, currency, depreciation of currency, paper, bullion, rates of exchange, value of precious metals in the market, and so forth; but looking down at the little chair, and seeing what a long way down it was, he answered: "Gold, and silver, and
30 copper. Guineas, shillings, half-pence. You know what they are?"

"Oh yes, I know what they are," said Paul. "I don't mean that, Papa. I mean what's money after all?"

Heaven and Earth, how old his face was as he turned it up
35 again towards his father's!

"What is money after all!" said Mr. Dombey, backing his chair a little, that he might the better gaze in sheer amazement at the presumptuous atom that propounded such an inquiry.

"I mean, Papa, what can it do?" returned Paul, folding his
40 arms (they were hardly long enough to fold), and looking at the fire, and up at him, and at the fire, and up at him again.

Mr. Dombey drew his chair back to its former place, and patted him on the head. "You'll know better by-and-by, my man," he said. "Money, Paul, can do anything." He took hold
45 of the little hand, and beat it softly against one of his own, as he said so.

But Paul got his hand free as soon as he could, and rubbing it gently to and fro on the elbow of his chair, as if his wit were in the palm, and he were sharpening it—and looking at the fire
50 again, as though the fire had been his adviser and prompter—repeated, after a short pause:

"Anything, Papa?"

"Yes. Anything—almost," said Mr. Dombey.

"Anything means everything, don't it, Papa?" asked his son:
55 not observing, or possibly not understanding, the qualification.

"It includes it: yes," said Mr. Dombey.

"Why didn't money save me my Mama?" returned the child. "It isn't cruel, is it?"

"Cruel!" said Mr. Dombey, settling his neckcloth, and
60 seeming to resent the idea. "No. A good thing can't be cruel."

"If it's a good thing, and can do anything," said the little fellow, thoughtfully, as he looked back at the fire, "I wonder why it didn't save me my Mama."

He didn't ask the question of his father this time. Perhaps he
65 had seen, with a child's quickness, that it had already made his father uncomfortable. But he repeated the thought aloud, as if it were quite an old one to him, and had troubled him very much; and sat with his chin resting on his hand, still cogitating and looking for an explanation in the fire.

CONTINUE

1

Which choice best describes the episode depicted in the passage?

A) One character receives a surprising inquiry from another character.

B) One character has an irresolvable conflict with another character.

C) One character reflects on decisions he has made over his lifetime.

D) One character admonishes another character about his aspirations.

2

Which choice best describes the developmental pattern of the passage?

A) A thorough analysis of an enduring convention

B) A detailed portrait of a meaningful conversation

C) A conclusive answer to a sequence of questions

D) A lighthearted reminiscence of a pleasant memory

3

As used in line 5, "entertaining" most nearly means

A) considering.

B) hosting.

C) regaling.

D) amusing.

4

For Mr. Dombey, Paul's questions about money are a source of

A) qualified admiration.

B) complete disdain.

C) cheerful optimism.

D) noticeable uneasiness.

5

Which choice provides the best evidence for the answer to the previous question?

A) Lines 11-15 ("On one . . . silence")

B) Lines 29-31 ("Gold, and . . . are?")

C) Lines 47-51 ("But Paul . . . pause")

D) Lines 64-66 ("Perhaps . . . uncomfortable")

6

Which of the following best summarizes the meaning of the "fire" as understood by Paul?

A) Clarification

B) Poetry

C) Sympathy

D) Practicality

7

The main purpose of the first paragraph is to

A) explain a family tradition.

B) identify two unlike characters.

C) describe physical oddities.

D) recapitulate an important event.

8

Ultimately, in response to Paul's questions about what money can do, Mr. Dombey

A) fails to supply answers that his son finds satisfactory.

B) becomes angry and scolds his son for being insolent.

C) embraces his son in a way that Paul finds reassuring.

D) changes the subject in order to distract his son from his sadness.

9

Which choice provides the best evidence for the answer to the previous question?

A) Lines 34-35 ("Heaven . . . father's!")

B) Lines 42-43 ("Mr. Dombey . . . head")

C) Lines 44-46 ("He took . . . so")

D) Lines 66-69 ("But he . . . fire")

10

As used in line 55, "observing" most nearly means

A) overseeing.

B) monitoring.

C) noting.

D) conforming to.

CONTINUE

Questions 11-21 are based on the following passage and supplementary material.

This passage is adapted from a recent essay by Jeremy Neill, "When Self-Esteem Loses Steam."

It seems counter-intuitive to argue that self-esteem would not be immediately beneficial for students. In fact, in psychologist Abraham Maslow's famous "hierarchy of needs"
Line (which ranks individual needs, including such basics as sleep
5 and sustenance), self-esteem is placed second. Maslow thought of it as being foundational for self-actualization, which is the highest human need in his system: no wonder self-esteem would one day become a guiding principle of American education. Starting in the 1970s, the proponents of the then-new
10 "self-esteem movement" claimed that positive self-image leads to increases in academic performance.

Even though the self-esteem movement continues to this day, self-esteem is not without its detractors. One of the leading skeptics is Roy Baumeister, a professor of psychology
15 whose research demonstrates a simple truth: self-esteem has been promoted without cause, based on one of the most fundamental flaws in logic. Baumeister began following the self-esteem movement in 1973, only to conclude in 2005 that "a generation—and many millions of dollars—later, it turns out
20 we may have been mistaken." Real evidence simply does not support the claims made by self-esteem proponents.

Among the many objections that have been lobbed at the self-esteem movement is the vague nature of the word itself. "Self-esteem" can cover positive personality traits like self-
25 worth, but can also describe disorders like narcissism. And self-esteem research is notoriously spotty. In 1989, a California self-esteem task force published a report which claimed that "many, if not most, of the major problems plaguing society have roots in the low self-esteem of many of the people who
30 make up society"—with very little evidence to back up this far-reaching claim.

Perhaps the greatest liability of self-esteem research is that many findings are based on self-reporting, which is often a very inaccurate method of collecting statistics. (People can, after all,
35 be terrible judges of their own personalities and behaviors.) Yet Baumeister wanted to conduct research that produced reliable numbers. He set out to find evidence to either prove or disprove the linkage between self-esteem and academic success in American schools. What he found was unexpected, at least for
40 anyone under the sway of the self-esteem movement.

Far from finding self-esteem to be a benefit in the classroom, Baumeister found significant evidence that self-esteem can actually be tremendously harmful. For example, in one study, students who received self-esteem-boosting
45 messages performed significantly worse on tests than did control group students who didn't receive the messages. More research needs to be done, but this revelation suggests the troubling conclusion that an emphasis on self-esteem has set America's educational system back significantly.

50 Baumeister's data suggest that self-esteem is a result of academic success, not the cause of it. The broader implication is that the entire self-esteem movement was based on one of the most basic errors in logic: confusing correlation with causation. Simply put, just because two things are related (such as self-
55 esteem and academic success), you cannot assume that one causes the other.

Think of this scenario somewhat more abstractly. If A and B are somehow linked, it's an error to think that A must necessarily cause B. The reverse may be true, as is
60 demonstrated by Baumeister's data, which show that academic success leads to self-esteem, not the other way around. Moreover, there could be another factor (or even more than one) which causes both A and B.

There was one thing, however, that Baumeister
65 demonstrated as a clear effect of self-esteem: an increase in initiative, including a willingness to try new things, such as raising one's hand in class. Yet Baumeister has sharp words for anyone who believes that this quality of assertion is entirely positive: "Hitler had very high self-esteem and plenty
70 of initiative, too, but those were hardly guarantees of ethical behavior."

Self-Reporting of Academic Success and Self-Esteem

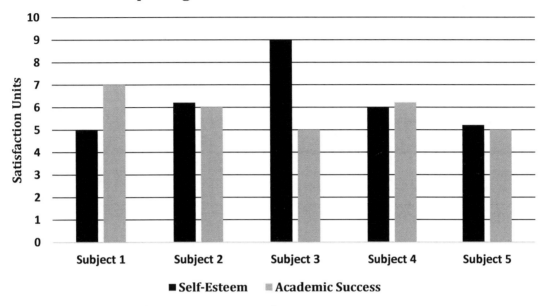

■ Self-Esteem   **▨ Academic Success**

11

Baumeister would most likely view the idea that self-esteem should be "a guiding principle of American education" (lines 8-9) as

A) unsubstantiated.
B) accurate.
C) perplexing.
D) duplicitous.

12

The author most likely includes Baumeister's comment in lines 69-71 ("Hitler . . . behavior") in order to show that

A) even famous figures struggle with self-esteem from an early age.
B) having self-esteem does not equate to a guaranteed positive outcome.
C) increased self-esteem often leads one to make poor choices.
D) self-esteem is directly correlated to the likelihood of violently anti-social behavior.

13

According to the author, the problem with self-esteem research is that it is

A) impossible to conduct because there are so many variables.
B) unfairly discredited because people are often the best judges of themselves.
C) unreliable because people often cannot gauge their own dispositions.
D) always slightly skewed because there is no absolute means of measuring self-esteem.

14

Which choice provides the best evidence for the answer to the previous question?

A) Lines 12-13 ("Even . . . detractors")
B) Lines 22-23 ("Among . . . itself")
C) Lines 32-34 ("Perhaps . . . statistics")
D) Lines 41-43 ("Far from . . . harmful")

CONTINUE

83

15

As used in line 22, "lobbed at" most nearly means

A) directed towards.

B) propelled towards.

C) tossed at.

D) deflected from.

16

According to the passage, the word "self-esteem" has

A) one overarching definition.

B) been misused throughout history.

C) created a society that is remarkably self-absorbed.

D) both negative and positive connotations.

17

Which choice provides the best evidence for the answer to the previous question?

A) Lines 1-2 ("It seems . . . students")

B) Lines 24-25 ("Self-esteem . . . narcissism")

C) Lines 37-39 ("He set out . . . schools")

D) Lines 51-53 ("The broader . . . causation")

18

As used in line 60, "academic" most nearly means

A) impractical.

B) studious.

C) school-oriented.

D) research-driven.

19

Based on the graph and passage, which choice provides support for Baumeister's argument?

A) Subject 1

B) Subject 2

C) Subject 3

D) Subject 4

20

According to the graph, which test cases provide support for the "self-esteem movement" (line 10)?

A) Subject 1

B) Subjects 2, 4, and 5

C) Subject 3

D) Subjects 1 and 3

21

Based on the passage, the author would most likely react to the information in the graph with

A) skepticism, because the findings are based on a research methodology with apparent flaws.

B) approval, because the data indicate that students are becoming critical of the self-esteem movement.

C) optimism, because the self-esteem movement is finding more reliable ways to measure academic success.

D) dismissal, because findings such as those in the graph are no longer taken seriously by most commentators.

CONTINUE

Questions 22-31 are based on the following passages.

In these readings, two authors consider recent innovations in skyscraper development and design.

Passage 1

Awe, wonder, and amazement at human ingenuity can all be sparked by the presence of a massive skyscraper. These buildings have the ability to impress and to convey a sense of
Line power. Yet the impulse to build ever-taller and more striking
5 buildings creates a paradox: the desire for immense height can lead to impractical design choices, but can also inspire technological innovation. In some skyscrapers, nearly 40% of the total structure is unusable space: these portions exist to make the building taller, but are not occupied. The desire
10 to make a striking impression can become more important than the desire for functionality, as when the top tiers of an impressive-looking cake turn out to be made of foam and cardboard, and are therefore inedible. The taller the skyscraper, the more likely it is to incorporate structures whose sole
15 purpose is to add height.

While the design and construction of skyscrapers undoubtedly reflect a human impulse to simply equate bigger with better, these buildings do in fact create opportunities for ingenious problem solving. The immense height of skyscraper
20 towers means that they face a nearly constant assault from wind, along with unremitting sun exposure. However, the choice of construction material is determined by aesthetic concerns as much as by practical ones. Along with a desire for height, there is also a strong demand that skyscrapers be
25 constructed primarily of glass. Glass, after all, heightens the visual impact of a tall building when the surfaces catch and reflect light, and also offers spectacular views. This demand has led to advances in glass manufacturing technology; according to Peter Weismantle, an architect specializing in super-tall
30 skyscrapers, "These days, glass isn't just glass." Glass panes can now be made larger and thicker than ever before and can be customized to accommodate building-specific needs, such as maximizing natural light while minimizing heat retention. These innovations may prove useful in fields other than
35 architecture, and may raise the possibility that skyscraper design can yield more than awe-inspiring buildings.

Passage 2

Sometimes more isn't really more: in many skyscrapers, the top floors are unusable space, there only to add height to the building. Other skyscrapers are paragons of spatial efficiency.
40 BIG, an architectural design firm based in Copenhagen and New York, recently won a competition to design a skyscraper for the city of Frankfurt, Germany. And BIG's skyscraper is the epitome of thinking outside the box—both figuratively and literally.

45 Rather than following the traditional rectilinear (or box) shape of most skyscrapers, BIG will shift the middle floors of its building laterally (or horizontally). The visual effect of shifting the floors relative to one another and relative to the majority of the building's space will be that the building will
50 somewhat resemble an elbow-shaped staircase at its middle section. The functional effect of the shift is that the middle floors will have outdoor terraces (on the steps of the "elbow staircase") where gardens can be planted. Similarly, the lowermost levels of the building will be shifted laterally to
55 create large terraces for public events.

Each of the building's three zones—lower, middle, and upper—has its own function. The lower floors will be used for gatherings and entertainment, the middle floors will serve as residential apartments, and the upper floors will
60 be used commercially as office space. "By gently shifting the floorplates of the simple elegant volume, the tower incorporates all the elements of a real city: spaces for living and working, inside as well as outside," said Bjarke Ingels, the head of BIG.

65 Despite its massive size, the building is meant to be inviting, not intimidating. "We want to create a new type of high-rise, a building that is open and approachable," explained Florian Reiff, BIG's senior managing director in Germany. The outdoor public terraces at ground level should help immensely
70 in that regard, but ultimately it is the fact that the building's large lower zone is dedicated to recreational use that will invite the public in.

22

As used in line 4, "striking" most nearly means

A) blunt.
B) prominent.
C) abhorrent.
D) eclectic.

23

It can be most reasonably inferred that the author of Passage 1 believes that

A) the high cost of building skyscrapers raises concerns regarding efficiency.
B) skyscrapers with even considerable amounts of wasted space may have more than just aesthetic merit.
C) a skyscraper's visual appeal should arise from its functionality.
D) the glass industry has contributed most to innovations in skyscraper design.

24

Which choice provides the best evidence for the answer to the previous question?

A) Lines 9-13 ("The desire . . . inedible")

B) Lines 13-15 ("The taller . . . height")

C) Lines 23-25 ("Along . . . glass")

D) Lines 34-36 ("These innovations . . . buildings")

25

As used in line 34, "fields" most nearly means

A) locations.

B) holdings.

C) disciplines.

D) structures.

26

Which of the following best describes the relationship between the two passages?

A) Passage 1 implicitly defends a practice while Passage 2 praises a specific example.

B) Passage 1 argues a single thesis while Passage 2 makes a series of concessions.

C) Passage 1 advocates a solution while Passage 2 harshly critiques a claim.

D) Passage 1 carefully describes a set of problems while Passage 2 thoughtfully poses questions.

27

The author of Passage 2 would most likely describe the "impractical design choices" (line 6) mentioned in Passage 1 with

A) reluctant acceptance.

B) apparent disapproval.

C) unreserved affirmation.

D) complete bafflement.

28

Which choice provides the best evidence for the answer to the previous question?

A) Line 37 ("Sometimes . . . more")

B) Line 39 ("Other skyscrapers . . . efficiency")

C) Lines 53-55 ("Similarly . . . events")

D) Lines 65-66 ("Despite . . . intimidating")

29

The information presented suggests that the authors of both passages agree that

A) building skyscrapers with large amounts of wasted space is ultimately more desirable than building unattractive structures.

B) tall buildings with large amounts of unused space fail to compensate for their inefficiencies.

C) the construction of tall buildings should be subject to increased regulation.

D) the practical concerns surrounding skyscraper design can lead to innovation.

30

The author of Passage 2 discusses the shifted middle floors of the new BIG skyscraper in order to

A) explain why the building will be difficult to construct.

B) contrast the efficient layout with those of BIG's other buildings.

C) assure readers of the building's overall safety.

D) highlight the principle that form should follow practical function.

31

Unlike the author of Passage 2, the author of Passage 1 is primarily concerned with analyzing

A) a breakthrough in architectural materials.

B) testimonies from practicing architects.

C) an aesthetic choice that has led to debate.

D) architectural projects that are funded by the public rather than by corporations.

CONTINUE

Test 5

Questions 32-41 are based on the following passage.

In the early 1950s, Senator Joseph McCarthy led a campaign against possible communist sympathizers in the United States government. McCarthy's fight against communist "subversion" has since been criticized as sensational and groundless. One of his earliest critics was Senator Margaret Chase Smith; this passage is an excerpt from the "Declaration of Conscience" that Smith delivered in the Senate in 1950.

I would like to speak briefly and simply about a serious national condition. It is a national feeling of fear and frustration that could result in national suicide and the end of everything
Line that we Americans hold dear. It is a condition that comes from
5 the lack of effective leadership in either the Legislative Branch or the Executive Branch of our Government.

That leadership is so lacking that serious and responsible proposals are being made that national advisory commissions be appointed to provide such critically needed leadership.
10 I speak as briefly as possible because too much harm has already been done with irresponsible words of bitterness and selfish political opportunism. I speak as simply as possible because the issue is too great to be obscured by eloquence. I speak simply and briefly in the hope that my words will be taken
15 to heart.

I speak as a Republican. I speak as a woman. I speak as a United States Senator. I speak as an American.

The United States Senate has long enjoyed worldwide respect as the greatest deliberative body in the world. But
20 recently that deliberative character has too often been debased to the level of a forum of hate and character assassination sheltered by the shield of congressional immunity.

It is ironical that we Senators can, in debate in the Senate directly or indirectly, by any form of words, impute to any
25 American who is not a Senator any conduct or motive unworthy or unbecoming an American—and without that non-Senator American having any legal redress against us—yet if we say the same thing in the Senate about our colleagues we can be stopped on the grounds of being out of order.
30 It is strange that we can verbally attack anyone else without restraint and with full protection and yet we hold ourselves above the same type of criticism here on the Senate Floor. Surely the United States Senate is big enough to take self-criticism and self-appraisal. Surely we should be able to take the same kind of
35 character attacks that we "dish out" to outsiders.

I think that it is high time for the United States Senate and its members to do some soul-searching—for us to weigh our consciences—on the manner in which we are performing our duty to the people of America—on the manner in which we are
40 using or abusing our individual powers and privileges.

I think that it is high time that we remembered that we have sworn to uphold and defend the Constitution. I think that it is high time that we remembered that the Constitution, as amended, holds forth not only freedom of speech but also trial by jury
45 instead of trial by accusation.

Whether it be a criminal prosecution in court or a character prosecution in the Senate, there is little practical distinction when the life of a person has been ruined.

Those of us who shout the loudest about Americanism in
50 making character assassinations are all too frequently those who, by our own words and acts, ignore some of the basic principles of Americanism:

The right to criticize;
The right to hold unpopular beliefs;
55 The right to protest;
The right of independent thought.

The exercise of these rights should not cost one single American citizen his reputation or his right to a livelihood nor should he be in danger of losing his reputation or livelihood
60 merely because he happens to know someone who holds unpopular beliefs. Who of us doesn't? Otherwise none of us could call our souls our own. Otherwise thought control would have set in.

The American people are sick and tired of being afraid
65 to speak their minds lest they be politically smeared as "Communists" or "Fascists" by their opponents. Freedom of speech is not what it used to be in America. It has been so abused by some that it is not exercised by others.

32

The main purpose of this speech is to urge the Senate to

A) be wary of those who preach communist and fascist beliefs.

B) uphold freedom of speech as a right that can be exercised without fear of persecution.

C) reconsider the Constitutional amendments that define freedom of speech.

D) take more of a leadership role in combating Communism.

33

As used in line 4, "condition" most nearly means

A) predicament.

B) ailment.

C) appearance.

D) background.

CONTINUE →

34

It can be inferred from the context of the passage that the reason Smith employs the sentences beginning with "I speak" in lines 15-16 is that she is trying to

A) stress the importance of eloquence when delivering a speech.

B) rise to a position of greater responsibility in the Senate by taking an assertive stance.

C) convey that she is in concord with other Americans despite her specific traits.

D) illustrate the various principles that define American individualism.

35

The example of the "non-Senator American" (lines 26-27) implies that

A) all Americans are valued equally, regardless of creed or ethnicity.

B) freedom of speech is afforded only to those who are wealthy.

C) in America, it is very easy for one to lose one's reputation and livelihood.

D) those not in the Senate are not given the same treatment as those in the Senate.

36

The passage suggests that

A) American society is on the verge of a national catastrophe.

B) the freedom afforded to Americans can easily be taken away by the Senate.

C) Senators occupy a privileged position above the other Americans in society.

D) it is very expensive to utilize the right to freedom of speech.

37

Which choice provides the best evidence for the answer to the previous question?

A) Lines 10-12 ("I speak . . . opportunism")

B) Lines 27-29 ("if we say . . . of order")

C) Lines 30-32 ("It is . . . Floor")

D) Lines 46-48 ("Whether . . . ruined")

38

Smith's attitude towards those in the Senate who cannot take the same criticism that they dole out can best be described as

A) contempt.

B) ambivalence.

C) confidence.

D) fear.

39

As used in line 44, "holds forth" most nearly means

A) recites.

B) upholds.

C) attacks.

D) lectures about.

40

The reason that Smith gives for why Americans do not speak their minds is

A) anger towards the government.

B) confusion about the laws.

C) engagement in peaceful protests.

D) fear of the repercussions.

41

Which choice provides the best evidence for the answer to the previous question?

A) Lines 18-19 ("The United . . . world")

B) Lines 36-37 ("I think . . . soul-searching")

C) Lines 57-61 ("The exercise. . . beliefs")

D) Lines 64-66 ("The American . . . opponents")

CONTINUE

Test 5

Questions 42-52 are based on the following passage and supplementary material.

This passage is adapted from Daniel Lee, "Tsunamis in Alaska? Past Research Sheds Light on an Ongoing Force of Nature."

A group of geological surveyors arrived in the wilderness outside of Juneau in 1952 expecting to determine whether petroleum reserves lie beneath the Gulf of Alaska. They
Line departed in 1953 preoccupied with a completely different
5 inquiry. At first glance, Lituya Bay, an eighteen square-mile fjord obscured by the Fairweather Mountain Range, appears to be the epitome of serenity. Untouched snowcaps and pockets of lush vegetation flank its reservoir of crystalline water; the scene looks rather like a painting, fraught with eerie stillness. Thus,
10 the team found it difficult to reconcile this apparent placidity with signs of destruction—uniformly scarred tree trunks, damaged rock formations, and sharply separated sections of young and old undergrowth—discovered around the waterline. What force of nature could have caused such marked damage at
15 such specific locations about the otherwise undisturbed bay?

In 1958, not even a decade later, a potential answer presented itself: a 7.8 magnitude earthquake caused a rock formation and its attached glacial material to dislodge and fall into Lituya Bay, displacing millions of tons of water onto
20 the opposite shore at over 100 miles per hour. The disaster decimated plant life as high as 1,720 feet above sea level and resulted in five human deaths, a mercifully small number thanks to the bay's remote location. Survivors' chilling eyewitness accounts prompted geologist George Pararas-Carayannis and
25 his colleagues to investigate the ability of subaerial impact events to trigger potentially devastating "megatsunamis."

Even the most cataclysmic ordinary tsunamis—sea waves resulting from the movements (generally earthquakes) of the sea floor—rarely reach heights above 100 feet. Unsure how
30 rockfall was able to produce a wave nearly twenty times higher, Pararas-Carayannis generated a scaled-down simulation of the event. Computer models of numerous trials revealed that, unlike a submarine tremor, a subaerial impact drags with it a burst of displaced air that forms a cavity under the water's surface.
35 Because air is less dense than water, the trapped gaseous matter escapes as an explosion of energy, further amplifying the force of the initial impact. As Pararas-Carayannis concluded in his 1999 report to the Tsunami Society, "the impact and the sediment displacement by the rockfall resulted in an air
40 bubble and in water splashing action that reached the 1,720 foot elevation."

The research presented in the Tsunami Society report suggests that the 1958 incident may not be isolated. Further examination of the age disparities among plants in different
45 sections along Lituya Bay's coast reveals that, while the most recent wave caused the most significant damage, at least four similarly massive rockfalls and accompanying splashes had occurred in the preceding century. Pararas-Carayannis confirms that what the oil surveyors noted during their 1952 expedition
50 was almost certainly the mark of a prior megatsunami: the loose rock deposits may even be in danger of plummeting into the water.

Because of Lituya's small size and secluded location, its potential to produce towering walls of water poses a negligible
55 threat to human life; however, some geologists interpret Pararas-Carayannis' analysis of the 1958 megatsunami as a micro-example of what could play out on a much larger scale. Specifically, Simon Day of University College London posits that Cumbra Vieja—the failing hotspot volcano on the African
60 coastal island of La Palma—is poised to shed 500 km³ of mass and send a wave capable of submerging New York and Boston across the Atlantic Ocean.

Despite the sound research supporting Day's apocalyptic prophesy, many are quick to point out its, as it were, faults.
65 Cumbra Vieja will almost certainly not fall apart all at once. "If you break up [a brick] into 10 pieces and drop them in one by one, you're going to get 10 much smaller splashes," Russell Wynn of the Southampton Oceanography Centre quips. While Pararas-Carayannis demonstrated that the theoretical destructive
70 force associated with megatsunamis is many times that of any tsunami in recorded history, the improbability that one will occur beyond the remote Lituya Bay negates the threat these forceful upheavals pose.

42

In the first paragraph, the author draws a contrast primarily between

A) a tranquil setting and evidence of past wreckage.

B) an ambitious endeavor and a disappointing result.

C) an inaccessible wilderness and signs of human activity.

D) the beauty of nature and the invasion of technology.

43

As used in line 23, "remote" most nearly means

A) unlikely.

B) isolated.

C) irrelevant.

D) reserved.

FIGURE 1

Tsunami Statistics

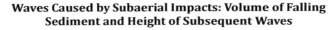

	Submarine Tremor		Subaerial Impact	
Magnitude of Earthquake	Miles Per Hour (MPH) of Wave	Impact (feet above sea level)	Miles Per Hour (MPH) of Wave	Impact (feet above sea level)
6.5	52	64	70	987
7.1	60	70	91	1230
7.8	82	100	100	1720
8.0	89	109	120	2012

FIGURE 2

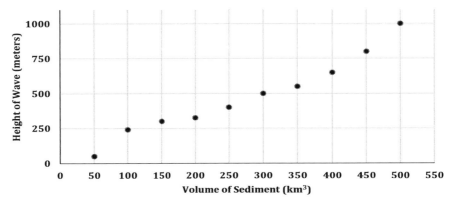

Waves Caused by Subaerial Impacts: Volume of Falling Sediment and Height of Subsequent Waves
Height of Wave (meters)
1000
750
500
250
0
0
50
100
150
200
250
300
350
400
450
500
550
Volume of Sediment (km³)

44

The passage indicates that Pararas-Carayannis and his colleagues were motivated to do their research primarily by

A) the mystery of what caused the tsunami at Lituya Bay, and whether it is likely to happen again.

B) a desire for recognition and respect among the scientific community.

C) the imminent danger to human life posed by the Lituya Bay.

D) an interest in confirming the observations of the geological surveyors who first noticed signs of damage to the coastline of Lituya Bay.

45

Which choice provides the best evidence for the answer to the previous question?

A) Lines 23-26 ("Survivors' . . . megatsunamis")

B) Lines 37-41 ("As Pararas-Carayannis . . . elevation")

C) Lines 42-43 ("The research . . . be isolated")

D) Lines 48-52 ("Pararas-Carayannis . . . water")

46

As used in line 60, "shed" most nearly means

A) streamline.

B) diminish.

C) release.

D) unburden.

CONTINUE

47

The final paragraph indicates that Simon Day's prediction about Cumbra Vieja is primarily

A) startling.

B) unfounded.

C) hypothetical.

D) destructive.

48

It can be inferred from the passage that submarine tremors

A) were not the likely cause of the tsunami in Lituya Bay.

B) cause the most damage at elevations higher than 1000 feet above sea level.

C) never cause waves that are faster than 70 miles per hour.

D) have weaker effects on the movement of water than subaerial impacts.

49

The author would most likely attribute the difference in height of impact between submarine tremors and subaerial impacts as represented in Figure 1 to

A) the relative size of the rockfalls during each individual tsunami.

B) the air pocket that is formed under the surface of the water during subaerial impacts.

C) the volume of the existing body of water where the tsunami occurred.

D) the magnitude of the earthquake that caused the subaerial impact.

50

Which choice provides the best evidence for the answer to the previous question?

A) Lines 16-19 ("In 1958 . . . Lituya Bay")

B) Lines 29-32 ("Unsure how . . . the event")

C) Lines 32-34 ("Computer models . . . surface")

D) Lines 43-48 ("Further examination . . . century")

51

In Figure 1, at what magnitude earthquake do submarine tremors cause tsunamis with an impact exceeding 100 feet above sea level?

A) 6.5

B) 7.1

C) 7.8

D) 8.0

52

Do the data in Figure 2 provide support for Russell Wynn's claim?

A) Yes, because the data show that large landmasses tend to break into small pieces rather than fall in one large chunk.

B) Yes, because the data show that the sediments with smaller volumes cause waves with smaller heights.

C) No, because the data reveal that falling sediments with large volumes are capable of causing massive tsunamis.

D) No, because the data do not indicate what caused the sediments to fall.

STOP

If you finish before time is called, you may check your work on this section only.

Do not turn to any other section.

Answer Key: TEST 5

Test 5

PASSAGE 1
Fiction

1.   A
2.   B
3.   A
4.   D
5.   D
6.   A
7.   B
8.   A
9.   D
10. C

PASSAGE 2
Social Science

11. A
12. B
13. C
14. C
15. A
16. D
17. B
18. C
19. C
20. B
21. A

PASSAGE 3
Natural Science 1

22. B
23. B
24. D
25. C
26. A
27. B
28. A
29. D
30. D
31. A

PASSAGE 4
Global Conversation

32. B
33. A
34. C
35. D
36. C
37. C
38. A
39. B
40. D
41. D

PASSAGE 5
Natural Science 2

42. A
43. B
44. A
45. A
46. C
47. C
48. D
49. B
50. C
51. D
52. B

Once you have determined how many questions
you answered correctly, consult the chart on Page 174
to determine your **SAT Reading Test score.**

Please visit **ies2400.com/answers** for answer explanations.

Post-Test Analysis

This post-test analysis is essential if you want to see an improvement on your next test. Possible reasons for errors on the five passages in this test are listed here. Place check marks next to the types of errors that pertain to you, or write your own types of errors in the blank spaces.

TIMING AND ACCURACY

◇   Spent too long reading individual passages
◇   Spent too long answering each question
◇   Spent too long on a few difficult questions
◇   Felt rushed and made silly mistakes or random errors
◇   Unable to work quickly using textual evidence and POE

Other: _____

APPROACHING THE PASSAGES AND QUESTIONS

◇   Unable to effectively grasp a passage's tone or style
◇   Unable to effectively grasp a passage's topic or stance
◇   Did not understand the context of line references
◇   Did not eliminate false answers using strong evidence
◇   Answered questions using first impressions instead of POE
◇   Answered questions without checking or inserting final answer
◇   Eliminated correct answer during POE
◇   Consistent trouble with Word in Context vocabulary
◇   Consistent trouble with Command of Evidence questions
◇   Consistent trouble with passage comparison questions

Other: _____

> **Use this form** to better analyze your performance. If you don't understand why you made errors, there is no way that you can correct them!

FICTION: # CORRECT_____ # WRONG _____ # OMITTED _____

◇   Could not grasp the roles and attitudes of major characters
◇   Could not grasp the significance of particular scenes or images
◇   Difficulty understanding the author's style and language
◇   Difficulty understanding the tone, theme, and structure of the passage as a whole

Other: _____

SOCIAL SCIENCE AND
GLOBAL CONVERSATION: # CORRECT_____ # WRONG _____ # OMITTED _____

◇   Unable to grasp the overall argument or thesis of an individual passage
◇   Unable to work effectively with the specific data or evidence in a passage
◇   Unable to respond effectively to tone, structure, and vocabulary
◇   Difficulty working with the graphics and graphic questions in a Social Science passage
◇   Difficulty understanding the logic or methodology of a Social Science passage
◇   Difficulty with the style and language of a Global Conversation passage
◇   Difficulty with the main historical and political concepts of a Global Conversation passage

Other: _____

NATURAL SCIENCE: # CORRECT_____ # WRONG _____ # OMITTED _____

◇   Unable to grasp the overall argument or thesis of an individual passage
◇   Unable to work effectively with the specific data or evidence in a passage
◇   Unable to respond effectively to tone, structure, and vocabulary
◇   Difficulty understanding the significance of the theories or experiments presented
◇   Difficulty working with the graphics and graphic questions

Other: _____

TEST 6

Test 6

Reading Test
65 MINUTES, 52 QUESTIONS

Turn to Section 1 of your answer sheet to answer the questions in this section.

DIRECTIONS

Each passage or pair of passages below is followed by a number of questions. After reading each passage or pair, choose the best answer to each question based on what is stated or implied in the passage or passages and in any accompanying graphics (such as a table or graph).

Questions 1-10 are based on the following passage.

Adapted from Sherwood Anderson, *Winesburg, Ohio*, a collection of linked short stories originally published in 1919.

In her girlhood and young womanhood Elizabeth had tried to be a real adventurer in life. At eighteen life had so gripped her that she was no longer full of illusions but, although she
Line had a half dozen admirers before she married Tom Willard, she
5 had never entered upon an adventure prompted by desire alone. Like all the women in the world, she wanted a real love. Always there was something she sought blindly, passionately, some hidden wonder in life. The tall beautiful girl with the swinging stride who had walked under the trees with men was forever
10 putting out her hand into the darkness and trying to get hold of some other hand. In all the babble of words that fell from the lips of the men with whom she adventured she was trying to find what would be for her the true word.
Elizabeth had married Tom Willard, a clerk in her father's
15 hotel, because he was at hand and wanted to marry at the time when the determination to marry came to her. For a while, like most young girls, she thought marriage would change the face of life. If there was in her mind a doubt of the outcome of the marriage with Tom she brushed it aside. Her father was ill and
20 near death at the time and she was perplexed because of the meaningless outcome of an affair in which she had just been involved. Other girls of her age in Winesburg were marrying men she had always known, grocery clerks or young farmers. In the evening they walked in Main Street with their husbands and
25 when she passed they smiled happily. She began to think that the fact of marriage might be full of some hidden significance. Young wives with whom she talked spoke softly and shyly. "It changes things to have a man of your own," they said.

On the evening before her marriage the perplexed girl had a
30 talk with her father. Later she wondered if the hours alone with the sick man had not led to her decision to marry. The father talked of his life and advised the daughter to avoid being led into another such muddle. He abused Tom Willard, and that led Elizabeth to come to the clerk's defense. The sick man became
35 excited and tried to get out of bed. When she would not let him walk about he began to complain.
"I've never been let alone," he said. "Although I've worked hard I've not made the hotel pay. Even now I owe money at the bank. You'll find that out when I'm gone."
40 The voice of the sick man became tense with earnestness. Being unable to arise, he put out his hand and pulled the girl's head down beside his own.
"There's a way out," he whispered. "Don't marry Tom Willard or anyone else here in Winesburg. There is eight hundred
45 dollars in a tin box in my trunk. Take it and go away."
Again the sick man's voice became querulous. "You've got to promise," he declared. "If you won't promise not to marry, give me your word that you'll never tell Tom about the money. It is mine and if I give it to you I've the right to make that demand.
50 Hide it away. It is to make up to you for my failure as a father. Some time it may prove to be a door, a great open door to you. Come now, give me your promise."

CONTINUE

Test 6

CONTINUE

1

The passage can best be described as

A) a brief description of a young woman's life followed by a significant dialogue.

B) a strident critique of small town social customs followed by an unflattering character portrait.

C) a discourse on the nature of marriage and the role of finances in family decisions.

D) description of how a young woman deals with untimely romances and an indifferent father.

2

The author indicates that Elizabeth sought the "hidden wonder in life" (line 8) primarily in

A) literature.

B) money.

C) travel.

D) romance.

3

It can be inferred from the passage that Elizabeth married Tom Willard because

A) he was a respected employee of her father's.

B) she was madly in love and could not be dissuaded from her choice.

C) she wanted to marry and he was a convenient option.

D) she needed a husband to manage the precarious finances of her father's hotel.

4

Which choice provides the best evidence for the answer to the previous question?

A) Lines 2-5 ("At eighteen . . . alone")

B) Lines 14-16 ("Elizabeth had . . . her")

C) Lines 33-34 ("He abused . . . defense")

D) Lines 37-39 ("I've never . . . gone")

5

The author indicates that many of Elizabeth's peers

A) had already been married and divorced by the time she considers marrying Tom Willard.

B) are mostly unhappy with their domestic arrangements.

C) have become comfortable with their situation as married women.

D) very meticulously catalogue the advantages of marriage for Elizabeth.

6

As used in line 33, "abused" most nearly means

A) assaulted.

B) insulted.

C) interrogated.

D) misused.

7

It can be inferred from the passage that Elizabeth's father offers her the eight hundred dollars because

A) his debts are substantial and he wishes for Elizabeth to be able to save some of her inheritance from his creditors.

B) he wants to help her and Tom start a life together.

C) he wants to atone for what he perceives as his poor parenting.

D) he wants Elizabeth to have some money to keep the hotel running after he is deceased.

8

Which choice provides the best evidence for the answer to the previous question?

A) Lines 31-33 ("The father . . . muddle")
B) Lines 43-45 ("There's a . . . away")
C) Lines 48-50 ("It is . . . away")
D) Lines 50-51 ("It is . . . you")

9

The tone of Elizabeth's father in lines 46-49 ("You've got . . . demand") can best be described as

A) apathetic.
B) insistent.
C) hostile.
D) accommodating.

10

It can be inferred that Elizabeth's father

A) caused Elizabeth to resent Tom Willard, but not to abandon the marriage.
B) believes that Elizabeth's considerable talents have been stifled by life in Winesburg.
C) did not successfully convince his daughter to leave Winesburg.
D) does not understand why Elizabeth intends to marry Tom Willard.

Questions 11-21 are based on the following passage and supplementary material.

The following passage is adapted from the article "Turbocharged: American Innovation and Its Discontents" by Larry Bernstein.

Do you have an extra $299? That's how much drivers in Maine need to pay in average yearly car repairs, which are necessitated by the poor condition of the state's roads and
Line bridges. And Maine is by no means the only state whose transit
5 has deteriorated; in fact, Maine is comparatively well-off. The national average U.S. motorists pay for repairs due to road conditions is $324. And yet, there is hope that our crumbling infrastructure can lead to something good.

But first, more bad news. Because infrastructure has been
10 in such bad shape for so long, the current cost of repairing the nation's roads and bridges is exorbitant. According to the Federal Highway Administration (FHWA), there is a chronic shortage of infrastructure funding and investment. Of the 600,000 bridges in the United States, one in every nine is
15 rated as structurally deficient, and the FHWA estimates that the nation must increase bridge investments by $8 billion to reduce this frightening number. Roads also require a significant boost in funding. The FHWA estimates that $170 billion in capital investment is needed on an annual basis to significantly
20 improve conditions and performance.

The consequences of continuing in this manner are grim. Gregory E. DiLoreto, President of the American Society of Civil Engineers (ASCE), notes that "most of us do not notice infrastructure until it stops working—when a bridge is
25 closed, when the lights go out, or when there is no water for your morning shower." Failing infrastructure is more than an inconvenience: it financially impacts everyone. As DiLoreto further observes, "unless we address the backlog of projects and deferred maintenance throughout the country, the cost to
30 each American family will reach $3,100 per year in personal disposable income."

The ASCE believes that if investment in infrastructure is not raised to levels needed for improvement, the American economy will pay a steep price. A 2012 ASCE report states that
35 by 2020, "the economy is expected to lose almost $1 trillion in business sales, resulting in a loss of 3.5 million jobs . . . the cumulative cost to the U.S. economy will be more than $3.1 trillion in GDP and $1.1 trillion in total trade."

A second 2012 report from the Building America's Future
40 Educational Fund details how individuals have suffered due to poor infrastructure. In 2010, Americans spent a total of 4.8 billion hours stuck in traffic, wasting 1.9 billion gallons of fuel, at a total cost of $101 billion. The report further explains that, relative to its economic competitors, the United States
45 has no national infrastructure planning, has systematically

CONTINUE

underfunded infrastructure investments, and has failed to use rigorous measures of evaluation and accountability for projects that have been funded.

In fact, former secretary of transportation Ray LaHood
50 has gathered statistics that show that our infrastructure is on life support: public spending on infrastructure has fallen to its lowest level since 1947 and the U.S. is now ranked 16th according to the World Economic Forum. LaHood adds, "you could go to any major city in America and see roads, and
55 bridges, and infrastructure that need to be fixed today."

That's the bad news. But there is a silver lining to all this: if the United States acknowledges the damages and aggressively re-vamps its infrastructure, the entire country could become a platform for transit innovation. Harvard
60 business professor Rosabeth Moss Kantor believes that the U.S. has a rich opportunity: "The investment would improve economic and social mobility by increasing access to a good education and jobs." In her vision, highways, bridges, tunnels, and city streets could become sensor-laden, interacting with
65 smartphones and vehicles over wireless networks. The sensors will provide better information and management, moving and re-routing autonomous vehicles before human passengers—formerly drivers—can even notice.

At times, Kantor seems to be imagining a country out of
70 a science fiction fantasy—except that she is a respected transit authority. Dynamic pricing (roads that charge higher user fees at times of high demand), more and better mass transit that is personalized, and hybrid-energy flying cars are also part of her vision. The question is whether Americans will look honestly
75 at their infrastructure, then look for ways to build a better system.

11

The main purpose of the passage is to

A) describe and debunk a common misconception about infrastructure.

B) introduce and explain a national problem that has the potential to be fixed.

C) detail a step-by-step process that will solve an international crisis.

D) criticize those who willfully ignore foreboding economic projections.

12

As used in line 3, "poor" is closest in meaning to

A) substandard.

B) immoral.

C) impoverished.

D) unlucky.

13

The passage indicates that repairing national infrastructure is extremely expensive because

A) there are so many bridges in disrepair.

B) the existing funds are not sufficient.

C) it has been allowed to languish for so long.

D) Americans cannot afford to pay for car repairs.

NATIONAL SPENDING ON INFRASTRUCTURE BY COUNTRY

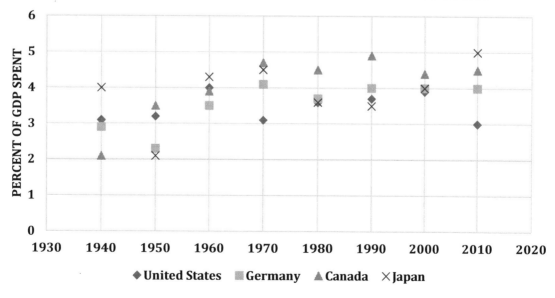

◆ United States   ■ Germany   ▲ Canada   ✕ Japan

14

Which choice provides the best evidence for the answer to the previous question?

A) Lines 1-4 ("That's . . . bridges")

B) Lines 9-11 ("Because . . . exorbitant")

C) Lines 26-27 ("Failing . . . everyone")

D) Lines 56-59 ("But there . . . innovation")

15

As used in line 34, "steep" most nearly means

A) sudden.

B) high.

C) vertical.

D) sheer.

16

The author acknowledges that visions for the future of United States infrastructure may appear to be

A) impossible.

B) all-encompassing.

C) convoluted.

D) unrealistic.

17

Which choice provides the best evidence for the answer to the previous question?

A) Line 21 ("The consequences . . . grim")

B) Lines 32-34 ("The ASCE . . . price")

C) Lines 69-70 ("At times . . . fantasy")

D) Lines 74-76 ("The question . . . system")

18

The fourth and fifth paragraphs (lines 32-48) function primarily to

A) emphasize the severity of a problem introduced earlier.

B) offer a personal perspective on the state of American infrastructure.

C) raise a counter-argument and refute it using statistics.

D) suggest a practical solution by citing respected studies.

19

How does the graph support the author's point about investment in infrastructure?

A) It projects the potential costs of failing to fix the existing infrastructure in the United States.

B) It highlights that Japan invests more of its GDP in infrastructure than the United States.

C) It demonstrates that costs to the citizen have skyrocketed in recent years.

D) It reveals that the United States is not a world leader in infrastructure spending.

20

In the graph, which country displays the steepest growth in investment during the periods 1950-1960 and 2000-2010?

A) Japan

B) Germany

C) Canada

D) United States

21

According to the graph, during which period were all four nations increasing their respective investments in infrastructure?

A) 1940-1950

B) 1950-1960

C) 1980-1990

D) 2000-2010

CONTINUE

Questions 22-31 are based on the following passage.

This reading is taken from an essay on recent developments in scientific research on disease and disease prevention.

For many years now, medical professionals have maintained that diets high in salt are unhealthy, due to the fact that such diets have been linked to high blood pressure, heart disease, and
Line various autoimmune disorders. A new study, however, indicates
5 that higher levels of salt in one's diet may also provide a positive boost for the immune system and aid in fighting off infections. If this new theory proves true, it could change the way doctors view sodium chloride.

The impetus for the study itself came when Jens Titze, a
10 clinical pharmacologist at the Vanderbilt University School of Medicine in Nashville, was studying the effects of salt intake on mice. Titze found that when the mice developed skin infections, high concentrations of salt would build up around the wounds. This was even true for mice that were put on low-salt diets.
15 Titze and his team hypothesized that the salt buildup around the wounds was a natural "first line of defense" put into place by the immune system. As Dr. Jonathan Jantsch, a microbiologist at the University of Regensburg in Germany, first put it, "we are salting our cells in order to protect ourselves."
20 In order to determine the exact mechanism behind "the salt defense," researchers focused on macrophages—those immune system cells in our bodies that engulf and destroy invading microbes. Jantsch and his team of researchers hypothesized that a salty environment might induce the macrophages to produce
25 and release "reactive oxygen species"—the molecules that are responsible for the destruction of invading pathogens. In order to test this theory, the researchers cultured macrophages from the body cells of mice, and added salt to the macrophage environments. The cells were allowed to grow until they
30 inhabited a solution with a salt concentration equivalent to the salt concentration found on the rodents' wounded skin. The results of the experiment were telling: the macrophages in the salted environment produced much higher levels of reactive oxygen species than those in the non-salted control group.
35 Next, the researchers added the common pathogen *E. Coli* to each group of macrophages. Within 24 hours, the density of *E. Coli* among the salted macrophages was less than half that of the *E. Coli* growing within the unsalted control group.

A final experiment was performed using the mice
40 themselves. For two weeks, the researchers fed one group of mice a high-salt diet, and another group of mice a low-salt diet. Then, the researchers infected the footpads of the mice with *L. Major*, a common bacterium. While all of the mice developed swelling and signs of infection, the mice on high-salt
45 diet generally healed much more quickly than the mice on the low-salt diet. Upon completion of the experiments, Dr. Jantsch

remarked that his results "demonstrate that extremes of salt intake result in additional salt accumulation in infected skin and boost immune defense experimentally."
50 Despite the success of Jantsch's experiments, many researchers in the field are cautioning against using the results to justify loading up on salt at mealtime. As Gwen Randolph, an immunologist at Washington University in St. Louis, noted, "The one thing that you don't want to take away from this study
55 is that it authorizes you to eat more salt to enhance immunity." While high-salt diets may have been helpful to our ancestors, the findings of Jantsch and his team do not erase the fact that salty diets have consistently been linked to medical problems such as cardiovascular disease—a condition that did not affect
60 prehistoric man.

Notwithstanding such reservations, the recent pro-salt evidence may find modern-day applications. While high-salt diets might not be effective remedies, topical ointments, gels, and balms high in salt could be developed in order to combat
65 skin infections externally, rather than from within.

22

The primary purpose of the first paragraph (lines 1-8) is to

A) establish the author's clear opinion on diets high in salt.

B) introduce a widely sanctioned statement that will then be contradicted.

C) provide context for an experiment that will be discussed later in the passage.

D) summarize the history of salt usage in the treatment of medical conditions.

23

As used in line 16, "put into place" most nearly means

A) relocated.

B) exhibited.

C) implemented.

D) prepared.

24

The passage indicates that a high concentration of salt was believed by researchers to help heal wounds by

A) accelerating metabolism in order to speed up the healing process.

B) sterilizing a wound and thus reducing the risk of infection.

C) strengthening the immune system by increasing the propagation of white blood cells.

D) producing molecules that aid in the eradication of microbes.

25

Which choice provides the best evidence for the answer to the previous question?

A) Lines 12-14 ("Titze found . . . diets")

B) Lines 15-17 ("Titze and . . . system")

C) Lines 24-26 ("a salty . . . pathogens")

D) Lines 40-43 ("For two . . . bacterium")

26

As used in line 32, "telling" most nearly means

A) revealing.

B) satisfying.

C) forceful.

D) shocking.

27

What is the main idea of the sixth paragraph (lines 50-60)?

A) Excessive consumption of salt has many unusual but innocuous side effects.

B) High-salt diets can do more harm than good to modern humans.

C) A high-salt diet is risky but can have significant advantages if properly administered.

D) Increasing the amount of salt in one's body can completely change the flavor of food.

28

Jens Titze would most likely react to Dr. Jonathan Jantsch's statement about salt intake (lines 47-49) by stating that

A) more experimentation is required before definitive conclusions can be drawn.

B) the results of Jantsch's experiment are consistent with his own observations.

C) the results of experiments on mice may not be applicable to humans.

D) the same results can be obtained even with low-salt diets.

29

The author refers to "topical ointments, gels, and balms" (lines 63-64) in order to

A) reveal how Dr. Jantsch was able to provide salt to the mice in his experiment.

B) list specific methods of salt intake that affect animals but not humans.

C) set forth examples of ways that salt can be utilized to heal wounds without negative side effects.

D) warn readers about products containing salt that seem benign but are in fact harmful.

30

The author of the passage would most likely agree with which of the following statements about salt?

A) Although high-salt diets were suitable for our ancestors, salt should be eliminated from modern diets.

B) Salt is a powerful antidote to many diseases and should be consumed more often.

C) A high-salt diet has many disadvantages, but is necessary for protection from pathogens.

D) Although salt can have healing properties, excess salt consumption is not advisable.

31

Which choice provides the best evidence for the answer to the previous question?

A) Lines 17-19 ("As . . . ourselves")

B) Lines 36-38 ("Within . . . group")

C) Lines 50-52 ("Despite . . . mealtime")

D) Lines 62-65 ("While . . . externally")

CONTINUE

Test 6

Questions 32-41 are based on the following passages.

Both of the passages below are excerpts from speeches delivered to groups of Native Americans by United States presidents. Passage 1 is taken from George Washington's 1796 "Talk to the Cherokee Nation," while Passage 2 is taken from Thomas Jefferson's 1806 "Address to the Wolf and the People of the Mandan Nation."

Passage 1

Beloved Cherokees, many years have passed since the White people first came to America. In that long space of time many good men have considered how the condition of the Indian
Line natives of the country might be improved, and many attempts
5 have been made to alter it. But, as we see at this day, all these attempts have been nearly fruitless. I also have thought much on this subject, and anxiously wished that the various Indian tribes, as well as their neighbors, the White people, might enjoy in abundance all the good things which make life comfortable
10 and happy. I have considered how this could be done, and have discovered but one path that could lead them to that desirable situation. In this path I wish all the Indian nations to walk. From the information received concerning you, my beloved Cherokees, I am inclined to hope that you are prepared to take
15 this path and disposed to pursue it. It may seem a little difficult to enter; but if you make the attempt, you will find every obstacle easy to be removed. . . .
Beloved Cherokees, you now find that the game with which your woods once abounded, are growing scarce, and you know
20 when you cannot meet a deer or other game to kill, that you must remain hungry; you know also when you can get no skins by hunting, that the traders will give you neither powder nor clothing; and you know that without other implements for tilling the ground than the hoe, you will continue to raise only scanty
25 crops of corn. Hence you are sometimes exposed to suffer much from hunger and cold; and as the game are lessening in numbers more and more, these sufferings will increase. And how are you to provide against them? Listen to my words and you will know.
My beloved Cherokees, some among you already
30 experience the advantage of keeping cattle and hogs: let all keep them and increase their numbers, and you will ever have a plenty of meat. To these add sheep, and they will give you clothing as well as food. Your lands are good and of great extent. By proper management you can raise livestock not only for your own
35 wants, but to sell to the White people.

Passage 2

My children, you are come from the other side of our great island, from where the sun sets, to see your new friends at the sun rising. . . . I very much desire that you should not stop here, but go and see your brethren as far as the edge of the great water.
40 I am persuaded you have so far seen that every man by the way has received you as his brothers, and has been ready to do you all the kindness in his power. You will see the same thing quite to the sea shore, and I wish you, therefore, to go and visit our great cities in that quarter, and see how many friends and brothers you
45 have here. You will then have traveled a long line from west to east, and if you had time to go from north to south, from Canada to Florida, you would find it as long in that direction, and all the people as sincerely your friends. I wish you, my children, to see all you can, and to tell your people all you see; because
50 I am sure the more they know of us, the more they will be our hearty friends. . . . We will provide carriages to convey you and a person to go with you to see that you want for nothing. By the time you come back the snows will be melted on the mountains, the ice in the rivers broken up, and you will be wishing to set out
55 on your return home.
My children, I have long desired to see you; I have now opened my heart to you, let my words sink into your hearts and never be forgotten. If ever lying people or bad spirits should raise up clouds between us, call to mind what I have said, and what
60 you have seen yourselves.

32

It can be reasonably inferred that Washington's ultimate goal for the Cherokees is that they will

A) travel across the entire nation on foot.
B) domesticate livestock and sell their surplus.
C) stop their violence toward other Americans.
D) maintain their tradition of hunting game.

33

Which choice provides the best evidence for the answer to the previous question?

A) Line 12 ("In this . . . walk")
B) Lines 16-17 ("if you . . . removed")
C) Lines 27-28 ("And how . . . them?")
D) Lines 33-35 ("By proper . . . people")

34

As used in line 12, "walk" most nearly means

A) follow.

B) hike.

C) escort.

D) resign.

35

Based on the passage, which choice best describes how Washington feels about previous attempts to improve Native American life?

A) They were numerous but largely ineffectual.

B) They were met with unwarranted hostility.

C) They failed because they were overambitious.

D) They were considered successful in their time.

36

The main rhetorical effect of the repeated phrase "my children" (line 36) is to

A) patronize and insult the audience.

B) establish an air of sympathy.

C) impose an economical hierarchy.

D) acknowledge the idealism of the audience.

37

In Passage 2, Jefferson wants his audience to travel across America most likely to

A) seek refuge from the harsh winter.

B) broaden their intellectual capabilities.

C) learn and apply modern farming techniques.

D) find camaraderie among other Americans.

38

Which choice provides the best evidence for the answer to the previous question?

A) Line 38 ("I very . . . here")

B) Lines 43-45 ("I wish . . . here")

C) Lines 51-52 ("We will . . . nothing")

D) Lines 52-55 ("By the . . . home")

39

As used in line 51, "convey" most nearly means

A) impress.

B) translate.

C) communicate.

D) transport.

40

Both passages are primarily concerned with the issue of

A) fostering modernization among Native Americans.

B) cultivating lucrative trade with the Native Americans.

C) forging peaceful relations with the Native Americans.

D) restricting Native American access to certain regions.

41

Which one of the following is mentioned in Washington's speech but not in Jefferson's?

A) Potential friendship

B) Exchange of goods

C) Former battles

D) Property rights

CONTINUE

Questions 42-52 are based on the following passage and supplementary material.

Launched into orbit in 1990, the Hubble Space Telescope creates high-resolution images of distant astronomical systems and formations. In this passage, an author considers the next generation of space telescopes such as the Hubble.

Are we alone in the universe? This question has tugged at the hearts and minds of children and adults, philosophers and astronomers, pragmatists and dreamers. The search for Earth-
Line like exoplanets (planets orbiting a star other than our Sun) has
5 always been a point of interest for humankind because of those planets' potential for extrasolar life (or life existing outside of our solar system).

Perhaps the most famous telescope is the Hubble Space Telescope. The Hubble has provided deeper and more detailed
10 glimpses into the far reaches of the universe than we have ever had before. However, many of those images are rather low-resolution.

The James Webb Space Telescope (JWST), which is scheduled to launch in 2018, represents the next generation
15 of telescope engineering. Unlike the Hubble, which uses ultraviolet and near-infrared wavelengths of light, the JWST uses mostly infrared light. It is also much larger than the Hubble, allowing it to peer more deeply and precisely into space.
20 Another, even more powerful, telescope has been proposed but not yet constructed. The Association of Universities for Research in Astronomy (AURA), an international group of astronomy institutions, has designed the High Definition Space Telescope (HDST). The HDST has an effective diameter
25 almost twice that of the JWST and is more than five times as wide as the Hubble's, which would enable it to provide images with much higher resolution. Marc Postman of the Space Telescope Science Institute commented that the "HDST would be able to detect features the size of the island of Manhattan on
30 Jupiter." Moreover, the HDST would be up to 100 times more sensitive than the Hubble to very faint light.

Both the JWST and HDST launches will utilize the L2 orbit, a region of space where the gravitational fields of the Sun and the Earth balance out. Gravitational fields behave
35 somewhat like magnets: the closer two magnetized objects are, the stronger the gravitational attraction between them, and the bigger the magnet, the stronger its pull. Imagine holding two magnets of opposite poles near each other. These two magnets would feel a strong pull towards each other. Now imagine
40 holding two magnets of opposite poles far from each other. The magnets would feel a much weaker pull towards each other. Because the Sun is more massive than the Earth, the Sun has a greater gravitational field, so that it pulls more strongly than the Earth does on objects. Thus, the L2 region is located closer to
45 the Earth than it is to the Sun. (The Sun is approximately 150 million kilometers away from the Earth, while L2 is only 1.5 million kilometers from the Earth.)

Once it has settled into the L2 orbit, the HDST may well revolutionize astronomy. "There is no area of astronomy and
50 astrophysics that HDST will not impact," said Mario Livio of the Space Telescope Science Institute. Livio went on to explain that the HDST would be able to provide images of dozens of Earth-like exoplanets and would allow scientists to study the exoplanets' atmospheres to see if they would be conducive to
55 sustaining life. "This will enable us either to detect extrasolar life, if such life is common, or at least place meaningful constraints on how rare extrasolar life is." Matt Mountain, the president of AURA, mirrored Livio's sentiments: "We hope to learn whether or not we are alone in the universe."
60 Ironically, the most pressing obstacle in getting the HDST built and launched may not be the astronomical distances involved, but rather the astronomical cost. The JWST, originally budgeted for $1.6 billion, ended up costing almost $9 billion, and the HDST is slated to cost roughly $10 billion.
65 The Hubble, however, was also a very expensive project in its day and was nonetheless successfully launched. Scientists, engineers, and space enthusiasts at large are optimistic that the HDST will overcome financing obstacles to provide us with new information about our distant surroundings, and perhaps
70 our distant neighbors.

Resolution of Orbiting Telescopes

Name	Resolution (arcseconds)	Mirror diameter (meters)
Hubble	0.05	2.4
JWST	0.10	6.5
HDST	1.50	12.7

42

According to the passage, the Hubble Space telescope is

A) the most advanced telescope available.

B) dependent on specific types of light.

C) similar to other telescopes in size.

D) less famous than other telescopes.

43

It can most reasonably be inferred that the primary purpose of the first paragraph is to

A) provide a psychological explanation for human curiosity about extrasolar life.

B) suggest that astronomers are similar to other people.

C) demonstrate the impossibility of extrasolar life.

D) introduce a question that may be possible to answer using telescopes.

44

The author compares gravitational fields to magnets in order to demonstrate that

A) the L2 gravitation is weak between the Sun and the Earth.

B) the polar orientation of planets affects gravity.

C) gravitational pull depends on distance and size.

D) the new telescopes bypass planets' gravitational fields.

45

Which choice best describes the author's attitude toward the future of the HDST?

A) The HDST is likely to overcome funding difficulties because the Hubble did.

B) The HDST's observations of exoplanets will contradict the JWST's observations.

C) The HDST will be abandoned because the JWST offers better resolution.

D) The HDST will need further design improvements to be feasible.

46

Which choice provides the best evidence for the answer to the previous question?

A) Lines 24-26 ("The HDST . . . Hubble's")

B) Lines 32-34 ("Both the . . . balance out")

C) Lines 58-59 ("We hope . . . universe")

D) Lines 65-66 ("The Hubble . . . launched")

47

As used in line 34, "balance out" most nearly means

A) become calm.

B) are equivalent.

C) seem insignificant.

D) weigh nothing.

48

It can most reasonably be inferred that the High Definition Space Telescope

A) is less sensitive than the Hubble.

B) has reached the L2 orbit.

C) exists only in design.

D) is the work of Marc Postman.

CONTINUE

49

Which choice provides the best evidence for the answer to the previous question?

A) Lines 8-9 ("Perhaps . . . Telescope")

B) Lines 20-21 ("Another . . . constructed")

C) Lines 30-31 ("Moreover . . . light")

D) Lines 62-64 ("The JWST . . . $9 billion")

50

As used in line 61, "astronomical" most nearly means

A) enormous.

B) intergalactic.

C) nebulous.

D) unlikely.

51

According to Chart 2, the resolution of the HDST is

A) almost the same as that of the JWST.

B) 10 times that of the Hubble Space Telescope.

C) about 3 times that of the Hubble Space Telescope.

D) more than 10 times that of the JWST.

52

Which of the following statements about the HDST is supported by both the passage and the figure?

A) The HDST is much more expensive than the Hubble Space Telescope primarily because of its larger primary mirror.

B) The larger diameter of the HDST allows it to capture higher-resolution images than other telescopes can.

C) The HDST's ability to provide images of objects far away in space will revolutionize astrophysics.

D) Although the development of the HDST is a breakthrough in astrophysics, the telescope will take many years to fund and complete.

STOP

If you finish before time is called, you may check your work on this section only.

Do not turn to any other section.

Answer Key: TEST 6

Test 6

PASSAGE 1
Fiction

1. A
2. D
3. C
4. B
5. C
6. B
7. C
8. D
9. B
10. C

PASSAGE 2
Social Science

11. B
12. A
13. C
14. B
15. B
16. D
17. C
18. A
19. D
20. A
21. B

PASSAGE 3
Natural Science 1

22. C
23. C
24. D
25. C
26. A
27. B
28. D
29. C
30. D
31. D

PASSAGE 4
Global Conversation

32. B
33. D
34. A
35. A
36. B
37. D
38. B
39. D
40. C
41. B

PASSAGE 5
Natural Science 2

42. B
43. D
44. C
45. A
46. D
47. B
48. C
49. B
50. A
51. D
52. B

Once you have determined how many questions
you answered correctly, consult the chart on Page 174
to determine your **SAT Reading Test score.**

Please visit **ies2400.com/answers** for answer explanations.

Post-Test Analysis

This post-test analysis is essential if you want to see an improvement on your next test. Possible reasons for errors on the five passages in this test are listed here. Place check marks next to the types of errors that pertain to you, or write your own types of errors in the blank spaces.

TIMING AND ACCURACY

◇ Spent too long reading individual passages
◇ Spent too long answering each question
◇ Spent too long on a few difficult questions
◇ Felt rushed and made silly mistakes or random errors
◇ Unable to work quickly using textual evidence and POE
Other: _____

APPROACHING THE PASSAGES AND QUESTIONS

◇ Unable to effectively grasp a passage's tone or style
◇ Unable to effectively grasp a passage's topic or stance
◇ Did not understand the context of line references
◇ Did not eliminate false answers using strong evidence
◇ Answered questions using first impressions instead of POE
◇ Answered questions without checking or inserting final answer
◇ Eliminated correct answer during POE
◇ Consistent trouble with Word in Context vocabulary
◇ Consistent trouble with Command of Evidence questions
◇ Consistent trouble with passage comparison questions
Other: _____

> **Use this form** to better analyze your performance. If you don't understand why you made errors, there is no way that you can correct them!

FICTION: # CORRECT_____   # WRONG _____   # OMITTED _____

◇ Could not grasp the roles and attitudes of major characters
◇ Could not grasp the significance of particular scenes or images
◇ Difficulty understanding the author's style and language
◇ Difficulty understanding the tone, theme, and structure of the passage as a whole
Other: _____

SOCIAL SCIENCE AND
GLOBAL CONVERSATION: # CORRECT_____   # WRONG _____   # OMITTED _____

◇ Unable to grasp the overall argument or thesis of an individual passage
◇ Unable to work effectively with the specific data or evidence in a passage
◇ Unable to respond effectively to tone, structure, and vocabulary
◇ Difficulty working with the graphics and graphic questions in a Social Science passage
◇ Difficulty understanding the logic or methodology of a Social Science passage
◇ Difficulty with the style and language of a Global Conversation passage
◇ Difficulty with the main historical and political concepts of a Global Conversation passage
Other: _____

NATURAL SCIENCE: # CORRECT_____   # WRONG _____   # OMITTED _____

◇ Unable to grasp the overall argument or thesis of an individual passage
◇ Unable to work effectively with the specific data or evidence in a passage
◇ Unable to respond effectively to tone, structure, and vocabulary
◇ Difficulty understanding the significance of the theories or experiments presented
◇ Difficulty working with the graphics and graphic questions
Other: _____

TEST 7

Test 7

Reading Test
65 MINUTES, 52 QUESTIONS

Turn to Section 1 of your answer sheet to answer the questions in this section.

Questions 1-10 are based on the following passage.

This passage is from Edgar Allan Poe, "The Murders in the Rue Morgue," originally published in 1841.

Residing in Paris during the spring and part of the summer of 18—, I there became acquainted with a Monsieur C. Auguste Dupin. This young gentleman was of an
Line excellent—indeed of an illustrious family, but, by a variety of
5 untoward events, had been reduced to such poverty that the energy of his character succumbed beneath it, and he ceased to bestir himself in the world, or to care for the retrieval of his fortunes. By courtesy of his creditors, there still remained in his possession a small remnant of his patrimony, and, upon the
10 income arising from this, he managed, by means of a rigorous economy, to procure the necessaries of life, without troubling himself about its superfluities. Books, indeed, were his sole luxuries, and in Paris these are easily obtained.

Our first meeting was at an obscure library in the Rue
15 Montmartre, where the accident of our both being in search of the same very rare and very remarkable volume brought us into closer communion. We saw each other again and again. I was deeply interested in the little family history which he detailed to me with all that candor which a Frenchman
20 indulges whenever mere self is his theme. I was astonished, too, at the vast extent of his reading; and, above all, I felt my soul enkindled within me by the wild fervor, and the vivid freshness of his imagination. Seeking in Paris the objects I then sought, I felt that the society of such a man
25 would be to me a treasure beyond price; this feeling I frankly confided to him. It was at length arranged that we should live together during my stay in the city, and as my worldly circumstances were somewhat less embarrassed than his own, I was permitted to be at the expense of renting, and

30 furnishing in a style which suited the rather fantastic gloom of our common temper, a time-eaten and grotesque mansion, long deserted through superstitions into which we did not inquire, and tottering to its fall in a retired and desolate portion of the Faubourg St. Germain.
35 Had the routine of our life at this place been known to the world, we should have been regarded as madmen—although, perhaps, as madmen of a harmless nature. Our seclusion was perfect. We admitted no visitors. Indeed the locality of our retirement had been carefully kept a secret from my own
40 former associates, and it had been many years since Dupin had ceased to know or be known in Paris. We existed within ourselves alone.

It was a freak of fancy in my friend (for what else shall I call it?) to be enamored of the Night for her own sake; and
45 into this bizarrerie, as into all his others, I quietly fell; giving myself up to his wild whims with a perfect abandon. The sable divinity would not herself dwell with us always, but we could counterfeit her presence. At the first dawn of the morning we closed all the messy shutters of our old building, lighting a
50 couple of tapers which, strongly perfumed, threw out only the ghastliest and feeblest of rays. By the aid of these we then busied our souls in dreams—reading, writing, or conversing, until warned by the clock of the advent of the true Darkness. Then we sallied forth into the streets arm in arm, continuing
55 the topics of the day, or roaming far and wide until a late hour, seeking, amid the wild lights and shadows of the populous city, that infinity of mental excitement which quiet observation can afford.

At such times I could not help remarking and admiring
60 (although from his rich ideality I had been prepared to expect it) a peculiar analytic ability in Dupin. He seemed, too, to take an eager delight in its exercise—if not exactly in its display— and did not hesitate to confess the pleasure thus derived. He

CONTINUE

boasted to me, with a low chuckling laugh, that most men,
65 in respect to himself, wore windows in their bosoms, and
was wont to follow up such assertions by direct and very
startling proofs of his intimate knowledge of my own.

1

Which choice best describes the developmental pattern
of the passage?

A) A nostalgic recounting of a close friendship
B) A detailed description of a forgotten part of Paris
C) A character analysis of a famous person
D) An explanation of the narrator's growing interest in
psychology

2

During the course of the first paragraph the narrator
focuses on

A) the social repercussions of a financial decline.
B) two contrasting views of the nature of poverty.
C) the depression caused by a substantial change.
D) the limited funds of an outstanding individual.

3

The narrator uses the phrase "whenever mere self is his
theme" in line 20 to refer to

A) a situation that is of special interest to people of a
certain nationality.
B) the humility that can result from frequently
discussing oneself.
C) a longer work that concerns the narrator's life and
family.
D) the narrator's extensive knowledge of different types
of people.

4

The passage indicates that the narrator was most strongly
drawn to Dupin because he was

A) interested in Dupin's life and lineage.
B) excited by the nature of Dupin's virtues.
C) amazed that they both had the same interests.
D) lucky to make a wealthy acquaintance.

5

Which choice provides the best evidence for the answer to
the previous question?

A) Lines 10-11 ("he managed . . . life")
B) Lines 14-17 ("Our first . . . communion")
C) Lines 18-20 ("I was deeply . . . his theme")
D) Lines 21-23 ("and, above . . . imagination")

6

As used in line 17, "communion" most nearly means

A) understanding.
B) contact.
C) religion.
D) affection.

7

As used in line 24, "society" most nearly means

A) company.
B) connections.
C) politics.
D) family.

8

When the narrator refers to the "sable divinity" in lines 46-47, he is explaining

A) how a guardian spirit watches over him and Dupin.

B) a third character who disappears before dark.

C) the characters' preference for nighttime activities.

D) how he and Dupin followed an admirably self-denying lifestyle.

9

The narrator implies that both he and Dupin prefer the night because

A) they can escape from the creditors that are pursing Dupin.

B) they are capable of speaking and writing with greater concentration.

C) they can quietly observe the city while they roam.

D) they live a secret existence that the night facilitates.

10

Which choice provides the best evidence for the answer to the previous question?

A) Lines 38-40 ("Indeed . . . associates")

B) Lines 43-44 ("It was . . . sake")

C) Lines 51-53 ("By the aid . . . Darkness")

D) Lines 54-58 ("Then we . . . afford")

Questions 11-20 are based on the following passages.

These passages feature perspectives from two authors who have written on quality-of-life issues among different age groups in the United States.

Passage 1

In 1900, the average life expectancy for Americans was less than fifty years. By the end of the century, that number was well over seventy years. In fact, since 1840, life expectancy
Line in the United States has risen about three months with each
5 passing year. And as average quantity of life increased, so did average quality. While people often face a period of very poor health before dying, that span has shrunk, due mostly to medical advances. In the words of Harvard University Professor David Cutler, "Where we used to see people who
10 are very, very sick for the final six or seven years of their lives, that's now far less common. People are living to older ages and we are adding healthy years, not debilitated ones."

But all this must be taken in balance. Although average quality of life has increased, the short span before death can
15 be a harrowing period for many of society's most elderly—a time when quality of life, actually, is at its worst. In 2011, a National Institute of Aging study estimated that 25-30 percent of people aged 85 or older suffer from dementia. The authors further commented that dementia prevalence is expected to rise
20 dramatically with the aging of the population worldwide. And even super-elderly individuals who remain mentally sharp are likely to outlive their savings and investments. The National Care Planning Council notes that unforeseen expenses— home repair and healthcare in particular—cause the biggest
25 challenges, while unscrupulous housing and medical providers compound the problem by preying on the elderly.

These trends are depressing to many observers, and most depressing of all to the elderly themselves. It is no surprise, then, that cases of depression have spiked among older
30 Americans. While severe depression is not a normal part of the aging process, there is a strong likelihood that depression of this sort will occur when other debilitating health conditions are present. And even healthy elderly are vulnerable: one third of widows and widowers meet criteria for depression during
35 the first month after the death of a spouse and half of these individuals remain clinically depressed for one year.

Passage 2

America is, it seems, becoming a nation of the elderly. A solid 20% of the current American public was born between 1946 and 1964, the years that mark the beginning and the end
40 of the famous "Baby Boomer" generation. As these individuals retire, nursing homes and medical providers will be challenged to offer adequate care. And medical concerns could only be the beginning of grappling with a huge, once vital population

CONTINUE

group that is now passing into retirement, inactivity, and
45 eventual infirmity: the psychological costs of leaving a
dynamic job or a fast-paced lifestyle will surely be great for
aging Baby Boomers, many of whom have stayed younger
in body and spirit (though not, of course, in numerical age)
thanks to advances in medicine and nutrition.

50   On average, however, Baby Boomers have had the
benefits of relatively appealing jobs and relatively robust
savings and retirement accounts. Sadly, the same cannot be
said of the other American age bracket that has been getting
a lot of press recently: Millennials, or individuals born
55 between 1980 and 2013. Millennials are in many cases the
children of Baby Boomers, yet does this mean that the average
Millennial and the average Baby Boomer have ever enjoyed
anything like comparable quality of life? Not really. In many
professions, Baby Boomers continue to hold management
60 and executive positions, sometimes until the age of 60 or 70;
this phenomenon limits the ability of even the most talented
Millennials to advance in fields such as law, medicine, and
university teaching—the very fields that eagerly embraced
Baby Boomers decades ago. Remember, droves of Millennials
65 came of age in the catastrophically bad job market of 2000-
2008; many Millennials left these years disillusioned and
dispirited, sometimes burdened with student loans and
dependent on their parents for basic room and board well into
adulthood. The Baby Boomers have never been problem-
70 free, but neither have they had to deal with this brand of quiet
distress.

11

According to Passage 1, the rise in average life
expectancy for Americans

A) has consequences unique to the super-elderly.

B) is misleading because the added years are of poor
   quality.

C) comes with longer a period of illness before death.

D) does not account for suicides related to depression.

12

The primary function of the word "even" in Passage 1
(lines 21 and 33) is to suggest that

A) it is reasonable to assume that all elderly people suffer
   from depression.

B) healthy individuals often are overlooked during mental
   health screenings.

C) the loss of a spouse is a significant cause of depression
   in debilitated people.

D) severe unhappiness and depression are not caused by
   physical illness alone.

13

The authors of both passages would agree that

A) psychological illness is the primary problem faced by
   an aging population.

B) Baby Boomers have reasonably stable sources of
   income.

C) the increase in the elderly population is a cause of
   concern.

D) elderly people are victims of housing and medical fraud.

14

It can most reasonably be inferred that the author of
Passage 2 would respond to the statement about "average
quality" of life (lines 5-6) with

A) indignation.

B) enthusiasm.

C) indifference.

D) disagreement.

15

It can most reasonably be inferred from Passage 1 that the
elderly can expect

A) to maintain their accustomed lifestyles into old age.

B) to receive support from the government after retirement.

C) to be financially unstable near death.

D) to inevitably suffer from dementia.

16

Which choice provides the best evidence for the answer to the previous question?

A) Lines 1-2 ("In 1900 . . . years")

B) Lines 6-8 ("While . . . advances")

C) Lines 21-22 ("even . . . investments")

D) Lines 25-26 ("unscrupulous . . . elderly")

17

How would the author of Passage 2 most likely respond to the statement made in lines 27-28?

A) Millennials will become psychologically distressed after taking care of their aging parents.

B) Elderly people are much more susceptible to clinical depression than younger people.

C) Action must be taken to prevent Baby Boomers from retiring and consequently becoming depressed.

D) Younger generations are also negatively affected by increased life expectancy.

18

Which choice provides the best evidence for the answer to the previous question?

A) Lines 37-40 ("A solid . . . generation")

B) Lines 50-52 ("On average . . . accounts")

C) Lines 56-58 ("yet does . . . life")

D) Lines 61-63 ("this phenomenon . . . teaching")

19

As used in line 45, "costs" most nearly means

A) liabilities.

B) values.

C) expenses.

D) charges.

20

As used in line 62, "advance" most nearly means

A) rise.

B) propose.

C) increase.

D) accelerate.

Questions 21-31 are based on the following passage and supplementary material.

This passage is adapted from Danielle Barkley, "Trains That Float: The Coming Revolution in Overland Technologies."

In almost every area of contemporary life, an emphasis is placed on speed. Any possibility of doing something, anything faster is greeted with enthusiasm, and many technological
Line advancements are driven by the desire to increase expediency
5 and efficiency. Transportation, in particular, exemplifies this "faster is better" mentality. However, since air travel became commercially available, further development in high-speed travel has been relatively limited, since flight has remained by far the quickest way to get from one place to another. Why
10 bother with land speed?

Well, a few ingenious engineers have bothered, and have achieved a breakthrough in train transit. Now, the recently-developed "maglev trains" have the potential to become the dominant new form of high-speed travel.
15 The term "maglev" is a shortening of "magnetic levitation" and hints at what makes these trains unique. Rather than resting on metal tracks and being propelled by an engine (like a conventional train), a maglev train hovers, or levitates, just above the tracks. In order to do so, it relies on electromagnetic
20 propulsion. An electromagnet consists of a conductive wire (most often copper) wrapped around a piece of metal. When an electric current is introduced via a battery or another source, the current flows through the wire and magnetizes the metal. The maglev rail system applies this technology using three
25 main elements: an electrical power source, a series of metal coils embedded along the edges of a track (known as the guideway), and large magnets positioned underneath the train. When the electric current is flowing, the metal coils repel the magnets on the underside of the train carriage. This magnetic
30 force is powerful enough that the train levitates slightly above the track (typically at a height of between 1 and 3 inches). The power supply running to the guideway is then calibrated to create a system of magnetic fields that push and pull the train along: the supply input alternates so that coils shift between
35 magnetic polarities. As a result, the magnetic field in front of the train pulls it forward, while the magnetic field that pushes at the rear adds further forward propulsion.

There are currently two different forms of maglev technology: electromagnetic suspension (EMS) and
40 electrodynamic suspension (EDS). The former relies on a conventional type of electromagnetic activity, in which a power source is required in order for the coils to conduct electricity; here, the magnets are located on the undercarriage of the train. EDS, on the other hand, makes use of superconducting magnets
45 that can conduct electricity even after the power supply has

CONTINUE

been shut off. In this system, both the train and track are magnetized. While EDS-powered trains have achieved higher recorded speeds and have been shown to be capable of carrying heavier loads, the current is insufficient to trigger levitation
50 when these trains travel at relatively low speeds (less than 62 miles per hour). Trains operating on EDS systems must roll along on rubber wheels until these vehicles reach sufficient speeds for "lift-off."

Both varieties of maglev technology eliminate friction,
55 since the trains are not in contact with the tracks while in high-speed motion. As a result, the trains can travel extremely fast, with top speeds of up to 310 miles per hour. The train carriages are also engineered with attention to aerodynamic design to further maximize speed and reach each new destination as
60 quickly as possible.

21

The central claim of the passage is that

A) the notion that "faster is better" dominates our culture, specifically in the field of transportation.

B) maglev trains operate efficiently by eliminating friction.

C) the technology behind maglev trains has the potential to revolutionize high speed travel.

D) there are currently two different types of maglev trains.

22

As used in line 3, "greeted" most nearly means

A) introduced.

B) discovered.

C) welcomed.

D) reproached.

Energy Efficiency by Transport Mode

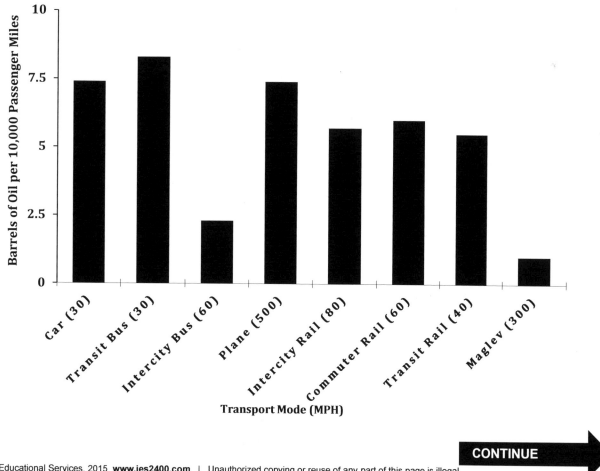

23

The main purpose of the passage is to

A) explain the mechanisms behind a technology.

B) discuss potential solutions to a problem.

C) reflect on the nature of innovation.

D) inspire future advancements in transportation.

24

The purpose of the first paragraph is to

A) illustrate the superiority of maglev trains.

B) provide context for the subsequent discussion of the passage's main topic.

C) describe numerous types of travel technologies before focusing on just one.

D) demonstrate a need for innovation by noting the problems associated with air travel.

25

As used in line 42, "conduct" most nearly means

A) usher in.

B) manage.

C) transmit.

D) comport.

26

It is most reasonable to assume that the author believes that

A) travel by maglev train will become more cost-effective than travel by plane.

B) the invention of maglev trains is one of the relatively few recent advancements in high-speed travel.

C) maglev trains are more successful in theory than in actuality.

D) current train infrastructure can easily be replaced by maglev technology.

27

Which choice provides the best evidence for the answer to the previous question?

A) Lines 2-5 ("Any possibility . . . efficiency")

B) Lines 6-9 ("However . . . another")

C) Lines 15-16 ("The term . . . unique")

D) Lines 54-56 ("Both . . . motion")

28

The passage most strongly suggests that

A) despite the superior performance of EDS-powered trains, their limitations make them too impractical for widespread use.

B) both EMS and EDS technologies will have myriad applications outside of transportation.

C) maglev trains will inevitably render airplanes obsolete.

D) the elimination of friction is the primary but not the only reason for the high speeds of maglev trains.

29

Which choice provides the best evidence for the answer to the previous question?

A) Lines 12-14 ("Now . . . travel")

B) Lines 38-40 ("There . . . (EDS)")

C) Lines 47-51 ("While EDS-powered . . . per hour)")

D) Lines 57-60 ("The train . . . possible")

30

According to the graph, which method of transportation is the second least efficient?

A) Maglev train

B) Car

C) Intercity bus

D) Commuter rail

31

Which statement is supported by the passage and by the information in the graph?

A) Due to their speed and efficiency, maglev trains have the potential to overtake planes as the new form of high-speed travel.

B) Transit buses use over fifteen times the number of barrels of oil that maglev trains do, but at only one-tenth of the speed.

C) Although maglev trains are eco-friendly and convenient, the cost of building them is too high for them to be beneficial or efficient.

D) EDS-powered maglev trains are superior to EMS-powered maglev trains in terms of both speed and cost efficiency.

CONTINUE

Test 7

Questions 32-42 are based on the following passage.

Early in 1986, Americans were stunned and saddened by the fatal explosion of the *Challenger* Space Shuttle. The following is an excerpt from the Address to the Nation that President Ronald Reagan delivered in response to this event.

Ladies and gentlemen, I'd planned to speak to you tonight to report on the State of the Union, but the events of earlier today have led me to change those plans. Today is a day for
Line mourning and remembering.
5   Nancy and I are pained to the core by the tragedy of the shuttle *Challenger*. We know we share this pain with all of the people of our country. This is truly a national loss.
     Nineteen years ago, almost to the day, we lost three astronauts in a terrible accident on the ground. But we've never
10 lost an astronaut in flight; we've never had a tragedy like this. And perhaps we've forgotten the courage it took for the crew of the shuttle; but they, the *Challenger* Seven, were aware of the dangers, but overcame them and did their jobs brilliantly. We mourn seven heroes: Michael Smith, Dick Scobee, Judith
15 Resnik, Ronald McNair, Ellison Onizuka, Gregory Jarvis, and Christa McAuliffe. We mourn their loss as a nation together.
     For the families of the seven, we cannot bear, as you do, the full impact of this tragedy. But we feel the loss, and we're thinking about you so very much. Your loved ones were daring
20 and brave, and they had that special grace, that special spirit that says, "Give me a challenge and I'll meet it with joy." They had a hunger to explore the universe and discover its truths. They wished to serve, and they did. They served all of us.
     We've grown used to wonders in this century. It's hard to
25 dazzle us. But for 25 years the United States space program has been doing just that. We've grown used to the idea of space, and perhaps we forget that we've only just begun. We're still pioneers. They, the members of the *Challenger* crew, were pioneers.
30   And I want to say something to the schoolchildren of America who were watching the live coverage of the shuttle's takeoff. I know it is hard to understand, but sometimes painful things like this happen. It's all part of the process of exploration and discovery. It's all part of taking a chance and expanding
35 man's horizons. The future doesn't belong to the fainthearted; it belongs to the brave. The *Challenger* crew was pulling us into the future, and we'll continue to follow them.
     I've always had great faith in and respect for our space program, and what happened today does nothing to diminish it.
40 We don't hide our space program. We don't keep secrets and cover things up. We do it all up front and in public. That's the way freedom is, and we wouldn't change it for a minute.
     We'll continue our quest in space. There will be more shuttle flights and more shuttle crews and, yes, more

45 volunteers, more civilians, more teachers in space. Nothing ends here; our hopes and our journeys continue.
     I want to add that I wish I could talk to every man and woman who works for NASA or who worked on this mission and tell them: "Your dedication and professionalism have
50 moved and impressed us for decades. And we know of your anguish. We share it."
     There's a coincidence today. On this day 390 years ago, the great explorer Sir Francis Drake died aboard ship off the coast of Panama. In his lifetime the great frontiers were the
55 oceans, and an historian later said, "He lived by the sea, died on it, and was buried in it." Well, today we can say of the *Challenger* crew: their dedication was, like Drake's, complete.
     The crew of the space shuttle *Challenger* honored us by the manner in which they lived their lives. We will never forget
60 them, nor the last time we saw them, this morning, as they prepared for their journey and waved goodbye and "slipped the surly bonds of earth" to "touch the face of God."

32

The main rhetorical effect of using a collective voice throughout the passage is to

A) create a bleak tone to describe a tragedy.
B) highlight the speaker's populist sympathies.
C) encourage the members of the audience to speak with one another.
D) unify the nation in a time of shared loss.

33

As used in line 17, "bear" most nearly means

A) endure.
B) uphold.
C) deliver.
D) form.

34

Reagan indicates that the particular nature of the *Challenger* tragedy is

A) inconsequential.
B) unavoidable.
C) unprecedented.
D) commonplace.

35

Which choice provides the best evidence for the answer to the previous question?

A) Lines 1-3 ("Ladies and gentlemen . . . those plans")

B) Lines 9-10 ("But we've . . . like this")

C) Lines 26-27 ("We've grown . . . just begun")

D) Lines 32-33 ("I know . . . happen")

36

Which of the following does Reagan indicate about the members of the *Challenger* crew?

A) They made an unfortunate mistake that resulted in the explosion.

B) They were knowledgeable about the risks involved with their mission.

C) They intentionally sacrificed their lives to contribute to scientific knowledge.

D) They possessed expert knowledge of space shuttle engineering.

37

What is Reagan's main point about exploration?

A) It is not inherently dangerous.

B) It is the only way for the country to move forward.

C) It is generally a field for daring individuals.

D) It very rarely produces results.

38

Which choice provides the best evidence for the answer to the previous question?

A) Lines 19-21 ("Your loved ones . . . with joy")

B) Lines 35-36 ("The future . . . to the brave")

C) Lines 43-45 ("There will be . . . in space")

D) Lines 59-62 ("We will never . . . face of God")

39

As used in line 36, "pulling" most nearly means

A) luring.

B) uprooting.

C) removing.

D) leading.

40

Reagan suggests that the space program's transparency is

A) reflective of the country's fundamental principles.

B) vital to the thorough education of schoolchildren.

C) a result of previous scandals regarding secrecy.

D) important in preserving its prestigious reputation.

41

Reagan mentions "Sir Francis Drake" (line 53) as an example of

A) an explorer who has often been discussed alongside the members of the *Challenger* crew.

B) a brave adventurer who perhaps dreamed of exploring space in his lifetime.

C) an idealistic man who was obsessed with discovering the mysteries of the ocean.

D) a pioneer with a commitment comparable to that of the *Challenger* crew.

42

It can reasonably be inferred that the "schoolchildren" (line 30) addressed by Reagan would

A) have been severely traumatized by the live coverage of the *Challenger* accident.

B) be unwilling to pursue science and exploration careers after witnessing the *Challenger* incident.

C) not immediately comprehend the idea that tragedy and advancement are linked.

D) be likely to misinterpret the heroism often displayed by astronauts as a form of recklessness.

CONTINUE

Questions 43-52 are based on the following passage and supplementary material.

The following passage is adapted from a 2012 article on lesser-known areas of study among biologists.

Cryptozoology is the study of animals whose existence is difficult to prove due to lack of tangible evidence. The first syllable of this word comes from the Greek word
Line kryptos, which means "hidden." Zoologists refuse to accept
5 cryptozoology as a part of their discipline, since for them it is a pseudo-science. They accuse "cryptids"—as the adherents of cryptozoology are unflatteringly called—of relying too heavily on anecdotal evidence such as legends and alleged but unproven sightings, rather than on physical discovery
10 or excavation. All of this skepticism and dismissal is rather galling to Richard Freeman, who runs the United Kingdom's Centre for Fortean Zoology, the world's largest full-time organization dedicated to cryptozoology.

Freeman believes that, in exploring how our present world
15 has evolved, it is essential that we do not disregard elements that scientists dismiss because physical evidence cannot be produced. He posits that the history of human presence cannot be defined only by debris that has been left behind in the ground or scratched in strange hieroglyphics on rocks or
20 pieces of dried animal skin. He points out that knowledge was handed down verbally from generation to generation well before writing appeared. Humanity's oral tradition cannot be dismissed simply as a reflection of man's imagination, for myths and legends speak of real and exact fears and threats.
25 Consider the dragon, which appears in legends around the world. Purportedly, there are three distinct species of this beast, with certain elements common to all. The Fire-dragon appears in European legend. It is a quadruped with bat-like wings, razor-sharp teeth and claws, and a mighty, scaly tail. It could
30 belch fire. It also possessed an uncanny ability to sense its prey across great distances. The second species, the Wyvern dragon, inhabited the oceans, had only one pair of legs, and possessed a venomous bite that could spread disease and pestilence. The third, the Lindorm of Asia, was an enormous, limbless reptile.
35 It spat venom or spewed poison gas.

The existence of dragons such as these has been dismissed by zoologists as fairy-tale thinking. However, such "fairy tales" can be found everywhere in Europe and China and Japan. Even in our present age, the presence of dragons is still reported, if
40 not scientifically confirmed. It is claimed that dragons have been sighted at Lake Nembu in Tibet and Lake Tianche in China. As recently as 1976, it was reported that a huge, winged reptile "terrorized" the population of the San Antonio Valley in the U.S. These claims have been countered by the "scientific"
45 argument that these were, probably, just abnormal varieties of Crocodile or Alligator or even exceptionally large Anacondas.

Yet, on the islands of Indonesia, zoologists have come across a species of reptile that is—possibly, they have decided—a development of the dinosaur Megalamia Proca,
50 which crossed from what is now Australia to Asia when these land masses were still connected roughly forty million years ago. This modern reptile has a scale-coated body and can weigh as much as 300 pounds. It has sixty serrated replaceable teeth. It is almost deaf and has poor vision and thus uses its
55 tongue to detect, taste, and smell. It sways its head from side to side as it moves, sensing the location of possible prey and carrion up to five miles away. It has loose, articulated jaws that allow considerable amounts of flesh to be torn from its prey and swallowed whole. This beast is known to eat birds,
60 monkeys, boars, goats, and human corpses. It can create both hydrogen gas and methane from acid accrued in its stomach— and these substances can be both venomous and flammable. The zoologists classify this animal as a very rare member of the Monitor family: the Komodo Monitor.
65 It was only when Sir David Attenborough pursued this Monitor for a BBC television nature program that the general public became aware of its existence. His film stunned all who saw it; cryptozoologists felt vindicated. Nobody calls this rare animal a Komodo Monitor. We know a Dragon when we see
70 one.

43

According to the passage, what is the relationship between cryptozoologists and zoologists?

A) Cryptozoologists defend their study of mythical animals as valid, while zoologists dismiss it as baseless and unproven.

B) Cryptozoologists and zoologists have a long-standing rivalry stemming from a debate concerning the existence of dragons.

C) Cryptozoologists are considered respected members of the zoologist community and are often in agreement with zoologists on various issues.

D) Cryptozoologists sometimes reach out to zoologists for assistance on topics such as evidence collection, but largely remain separate from zoologists.

CONTINUE

Sightings of Mythical Creatures in the 20th Century

Dragons ······ Bigfoot — — Loch Ness Monster

44

Which choice provides the best evidence for the answer to the previous question?

A) Lines 1-2 ("Cryptozoology . . . evidence")

B) Lines 4-6 ("Zoologists . . . pseudo-science")

C) Lines 17-20 ("He posits . . . skin")

D) Lines 20-22 ("He points . . . appeared")

45

The author indicates that the field of cryptozoology is important because

A) it would explain many of the sightings of mythological creatures throughout history and within the past century.

B) it helps people understand the history and progression of human beings and animals through evidence that is not purely tangible.

C) it allows scientists to research rare and unique species of animals such as the Komodo Monitor that would otherwise not be discovered.

D) it assists zoologists in their search for animals whose existence has been recorded but not confirmed.

46

Which choice provides the best evidence for the answer to the previous question?

A) Lines 14-17 ("in exploring . . . produced")

B) Lines 26-27 ("Purportedly . . . to all")

C) Lines 40-42 ("It is claimed . . . China")

D) Lines 47-50 ("Yet, on the . . . Asia")

47

As used in line 26, "distinct" most nearly means

A) noticeable.

B) unmistakable.

C) separate.

D) recognizable.

48

As used in line 63, "rare" most nearly means

A) extraordinary.

B) unlikely.

C) uncommon.

D) strange.

CONTINUE

49

The passage implies that cryptozoologists felt "vindicated" (line 68) because

A) the Komodo Monitor has features and characteristics similar to a dragon's, making the beliefs of cryptozoologists plausible.

B) zoologists regard the discovery of the Komodo Monitor as a breakthrough, although cryptozoologists had originally studied the animal.

C) the Komodo Monitor has been dismissed by scientists as a hoax, yet evidence and reports suggest otherwise.

D) cryptozoologists have requested funding for research on the Komodo Monitor for years, but money was given to established zoologists instead.

50

The author uses the word "we" in line 69 primarily to

A) reflect the sense of camaraderie among many well known and established cryptozoologists.

B) emphasize the need for unity between the cryptozoologist and zoologist communities.

C) establish a mood of solidarity and understanding within a small group of zoologists.

D) express support of a branch of science that some would consider questionable.

51

Based on the graph, reports of dragon sightings have

A) tripled from 1980 to 2000.

B) increased at a relatively steady rate.

C) decreased insignificantly.

D) decreased by more than 50% since the 1960s.

52

According to the passage, zoologists would most likely respond to the data presented in the graph concerning dragon sightings with

A) a consensus that the animals reported could be either dragons or some other mythological creature.

B) an agreement that the reptiles sighted have not been reported previously, but doubt about the existence of dragons.

C) an assertion that the creatures seen were more likely abnormal species of Crocodile or Alligator.

D) a contention that the people recording dragon sightings were merely seeking attention through a hoax.

STOP

If you finish before time is called, you may check your work on this section only.

Do not turn to any other section.

Answer Key: TEST 7

PASSAGE 1
Fiction

1.   A
2.   D
3.   A
4.   B
5.   D
6.   B
7.   A
8.   C
9.   C
10. D

PASSAGE 2
Social Science

11. A
12. D
13. C
14. D
15. C
16. C
17. D
18. D
19. A
20. A

PASSAGE 3
Natural Science 1

21. C
22. C
23. A
24. B
25. C
26. B
27. B
28. D
29. D
30. B
31. A

PASSAGE 4
Global Conversation

32. D
33. A
34. C
35. B
36. B
37. C
38. B
39. D
40. A
41. D
42. C

PASSAGE 5
Natural Science 2

43. A
44. B
45. B
46. A
47. C
48. C
49. A
50. D
51. B
52. C

Once you have determined how many questions
you answered correctly, consult the chart on Page 174
to determine your **SAT Reading Test score.**

Please visit **ies2400.com/answers** for answer explanations.

Post-Test Analysis

This post-test analysis is essential if you want to see an improvement on your next test. Possible reasons for errors on the five passages in this test are listed here. Place check marks next to the types of errors that pertain to you, or write your own types of errors in the blank spaces.

TIMING AND ACCURACY

◇ Spent too long reading individual passages
◇ Spent too long answering each question
◇ Spent too long on a few difficult questions
◇ Felt rushed and made silly mistakes or random errors
◇ Unable to work quickly using textual evidence and POE
Other: _____

APPROACHING THE PASSAGES AND QUESTIONS

◇ Unable to effectively grasp a passage's tone or style
◇ Unable to effectively grasp a passage's topic or stance
◇ Did not understand the context of line references
◇ Did not eliminate false answers using strong evidence
◇ Answered questions using first impressions instead of POE
◇ Answered questions without checking or inserting final answer
◇ Eliminated correct answer during POE
◇ Consistent trouble with Word in Context vocabulary
◇ Consistent trouble with Command of Evidence questions
◇ Consistent trouble with passage comparison questions
Other: _____

> **Use this form** to better analyze your performance. If you don't understand why you made errors, there is no way that you can correct them!

FICTION: # CORRECT_____ # WRONG _____ # OMITTED _____

◇ Could not grasp the roles and attitudes of major characters
◇ Could not grasp the significance of particular scenes or images
◇ Difficulty understanding the author's style and language
◇ Difficulty understanding the tone, theme, and structure of the passage as a whole
Other: _____

SOCIAL SCIENCE AND
GLOBAL CONVERSATION: # CORRECT_____ # WRONG _____ # OMITTED _____

◇ Unable to grasp the overall argument or thesis of an individual passage
◇ Unable to work effectively with the specific data or evidence in a passage
◇ Unable to respond effectively to tone, structure, and vocabulary
◇ Difficulty working with the graphics and graphic questions in a Social Science passage
◇ Difficulty understanding the logic or methodology of a Social Science passage
◇ Difficulty with the style and language of a Global Conversation passage
◇ Difficulty with the main historical and political concepts of a Global Conversation passage
Other: _____

NATURAL SCIENCE: # CORRECT_____ # WRONG _____ # OMITTED _____

◇ Unable to grasp the overall argument or thesis of an individual passage
◇ Unable to work effectively with the specific data or evidence in a passage
◇ Unable to respond effectively to tone, structure, and vocabulary
◇ Difficulty understanding the significance of the theories or experiments presented
◇ Difficulty working with the graphics and graphic questions
Other: _____

TEST 8

Reading Test

65 MINUTES, 52 QUESTIONS

Turn to Section 1 of your answer sheet to answer the questions in this section.

DIRECTIONS

Each passage or pair of passages below is followed by a number of questions. After reading each passage or pair, choose the best answer to each question based on what is stated or implied in the passage or passages and in any accompanying graphics (such as a table or graph).

Questions 1-10 are based on the following passage.

This passage is from James Joyce, "A Little Cloud." Originally published in the short story collection *Dubliners* in 1914.

Eight years before he had seen his friend off at the North Wall and wished him godspeed, Gallaher had got on. You could tell that at once by his travelled air, his well-cut tweed
Line suit, and fearless accent. Few fellows had talents like his and
5 fewer still could remain unspoiled by such success. Gallaher's heart was in the right place and he had deserved to win. It was something to have a friend like that.

Little Chandler's thoughts ever since lunch-time had been of his meeting with Gallaher, of Gallaher's invitation and of
10 the great city London where Gallaher lived. He was called Little Chandler because, though he was but slightly under the average stature, he gave one the idea of being a little man. His hands were white and small, his frame was fragile, his voice was quiet and his manners were refined. He took the greatest
15 care of his fair silken hair and moustache and used perfume discreetly on his handkerchief. The half-moons of his nails were perfect and when he smiled you caught a glimpse of a row of childish white teeth.

As he sat at his desk in the King's Inns he thought what
20 changes those eight years had brought. The friend whom he had known under a shabby and necessitous guise had become a brilliant figure on the London Press. He turned often from his tiresome writing to gaze out of the office window. The glow of a late autumn sunset covered the grass plots and
25 walks. It cast a shower of kindly golden dust on the untidy nurses and decrepit old men who drowsed on the benches; it flickered upon all the moving figures—on the children who ran screaming along the gravel paths and on everyone who passed through the gardens. He watched the scene and thought
30 of life, and (as always happened when he thought of life) he became sad. A gentle melancholy took possession of him. He felt how useless it was to struggle against fortune, this being the burden of wisdom which the ages had bequeathed to him.

He remembered the books of poetry upon his shelves at
35 home. He had bought them in his bachelor days and many an evening, as he sat in the little room off the hall, he had been tempted to take one down from the bookshelf and read out something to his wife. But shyness had always held him back; and so the books had remained on their shelves. At times he
40 repeated lines to himself and this consoled him.

When his hour had struck he stood up and took leave of his desk and of his fellow-clerks punctiliously. He emerged from under the feudal arch of the King's Inns, a neat modest figure, and walked swiftly down Henrietta Street. The golden
45 sunset was waning and the air had grown sharp. A horde of grimy children populated the street. They stood or ran in the roadway or crawled up the steps before the gaping doors or squatted like mice upon the thresholds. Little Chandler gave them no thought. He picked his way deftly through all that
50 minute vermin-like life and under the shadow of the gaunt spectral mansions in which the old nobility of Dublin had roystered. No memory of the past touched him, for his mind was full of a present joy.

He had never been in Corless's but he knew the value of
55 the name. He knew that people went there after the theatre to eat oysters and drink liqueurs, and he had heard that the waiters there spoke French and German. Walking swiftly by at night he had seen cabs drawn up before the door and richly dressed ladies, escorted by cavaliers, alight and enter quickly.
60 They wore noisy dresses and many wraps. Their faces were powdered and they caught up their dresses, when they touched earth, like alarmed Atalantas. He had always passed without

CONTINUE

turning his head to look. It was his habit to walk swiftly in the street even by day and whenever he found himself in the
65 city late at night he hurried on his way apprehensively and excitedly.

1

The first paragraph primarily suggests that Gallaher is

A) disingenuous.
B) generous.
C) exceptional.
D) cautious.

2

In the second paragraph, the narrator makes a distinction between

A) appearance and reality.
B) height and demeanor.
C) intention and behavior.
D) precision and carelessness.

3

As used in line 24, "plots" most nearly means

A) diagrams.
B) actions.
C) plans.
D) areas.

4

The effect of the parenthetical phrase in line 30 is to

A) emphasize the gloomy nature of life.
B) suggest the reliability of a response.
C) indicate an unhealthy obsession.
D) imply that an emotion is unexpected.

5

The children in the passage are portrayed primarily as

A) surprising.
B) joyful.
C) inconsequential.
D) innocent.

6

Which choice provides the best evidence for the answer to the previous question?

A) Lines 16-18 ("The half-moons . . . white teeth")
B) Lines 26-29 ("it flickered . . . the gardens")
C) Lines 45-46 ("A horde . . . the street")
D) Lines 48-49 ("Little Chandler . . . thought")

7

As used in line 45, "sharp" most nearly means

A) caustic.
B) shrill.
C) crisp.
D) acute.

8

It can be inferred from the passage that Corless's

A) has a distinctive reputation.
B) is of no interest to Little Chandler.
C) is isolated from the outside world.
D) takes pride in its international audience.

9

Which choice provides the best evidence for the answer to the previous question?

A) Lines 54-55 ("He had . . . the name")
B) Lines 55-57 ("He knew . . . German")
C) Lines 60-62 ("Their faces . . . Atlantas")
D) Lines 62-66 ("He had . . . excitedly")

10

It can be inferred from the passage that Gallaher

A) has abandoned his friend.
B) has become a successful man.
C) has known Little Chandler since childhood.
D) is not especially well educated.

CONTINUE ➡ 129

Questions 11-21 are based on the following passage and supplementary material.

The following passage is adapted from the article "Advertiser's Remorse: Marketing Trends That Won't Go Away" by Cynthia Helzner.

Obesity, particularly childhood obesity, is a growing epidemic. Over the long term, obesity increases a person's risk of diabetes, cancer, cardiovascular disease, asthma,
Line sleep apnea, and joint dysfunction. Because all these risks
5 are associated with childhood obesity—the start of unhealthy behaviors—many parents, educators, researchers, and medical professionals have become concerned about the extent to which unhealthy foods are advertised to children.

Fast food companies in particular have come under
10 scrutiny for unethical business practices regarding marketing to children (since, after all, less than 1% of kids' combo meals are classified as healthy). An open letter from health professionals to McDonald's reads: "In the decades to come, one in three children will develop type 2 diabetes as a result of diets high
15 in McDonald's-style junk food, according to the Centers for Disease Control and Prevention. This generation of children may be the first in U.S. history to live shorter lives than their parents."

Furthermore, a recent study published in the Journal of
20 the American Dietetic Association reveals that unhealthy foods are represented in a disproportionately large number of TV advertisements. The authors of the study analyzed commercials shown in 90 hours of television and found that the majority of food ads were for fast food. The researchers then calculated
25 that consuming only the foods advertised would result in a diet with 122% more cholesterol, 137% more saturated fat, 162% more salt, and a whopping 2400% more sugar than the USDA (US Department of Agriculture) recommends. In contrast, a person on such a diet would consume 50% of the recommended
30 amounts of calcium, B vitamins, and vitamin D, less than half of the recommended amounts of fruits and vegetables, and only 5% of the amount of fiber recommended by the USDA.

So, fast food is unhealthy, but the ethics of fast food advertising are not unambiguous. It can be argued, after
35 all, that every company has a right to advertise in order to increase its profits. Yet children are generally much more impressionable than adults and many have not developed the ability to weigh factors such as health against their immediate desires for snacks and toys. Moreover, a child viewing an ad
40 in which children are having fun playing with happy meal toys may not realize that the children in the ad are being paid to pretend to be having fun.

A report by Yale University's Rudd Center for Food Policy and Obesity even found that fast food companies spend
45 most of their advertising budgets on advertising the toys that come with children's meals. McDonald's in particular has come under fire for advertising happy meal toys and for using Ronald McDonald as its mascot in an effort to sway children into wanting unhealthy happy meals. Even as other restaurants
50 have decreased their budgets for ads targeting kids, fast food chains have largely continued to increase their spending on ads aimed at minors. In particular, fast food ad viewership by teens on social media has skyrocketed. Even though some healthy options are available (e.g. apple slices instead of French
55 fries), ad spending to promote those healthy options has not increased.

If these practices are unethical and attract public scrutiny, why do fast food chains continue to advertise so heavily to children? The simple answer is: it works. Multiple studies
60 have found a positive correlation between the number of hours of television watched and a child's BMI (Body Mass Index, which is a measure of how much of a person's body is made of fat). Studies have also shown that a ban on such ads would reduce the incidence of overweight and obese children.
65 In 2008, the United Kingdom introduced a ban on advertising foods high in fat, sodium, and sugar to children. In contrast, the U.S. does not have such a ban. Rather, companies self-regulate under the oversight of the Better Business Bureau. Judging by the content of the ads (some so unethical
70 that they have been pulled from circulation), self-regulation does not seem to be working; stricter regulations are needed to protect the health of our youth.

Fast Food Ads Viewed by Different Age Groups

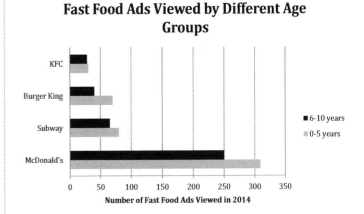

11

The main point of the passage is to

A) detail the consequences of an epidemic.

B) describe the benefits of a practice.

C) caution against unhealthy behaviors.

D) establish the need for a certain type of reform.

CONTINUE

12

The first paragraph serves to

A) assess the relative merits of an activity.

B) express concern about a predictable process.

C) describe the reasons behind a specific concern.

D) introduce differing opinions about an argument.

13

As used in line 34, the phrase "not unambiguous" most nearly means

A) easily overlooked.

B) glaringly obvious.

C) almost incomprehensible.

D) somewhat complicated.

14

The author of the passage suggests that marketing fast food to children is

A) commendable and successful.

B) misguided and impractical.

C) effective but deplorable.

D) comical but dangerous.

15

Which choice provides the best evidence for the answer to the previous question?

A) Lines 19-22 ("a recent . . . advertisements")

B) Lines 34-36 ("It can . . . profits")

C) Lines 52-53 ("In particular . . . skyrocketed")

D) Lines 57-59 ("If these. . . works")

16

It can be most reasonably inferred that the author thinks the United Kingdom's ban

A) is more successful than the policies that are prevalent in the United States.

B) is an abridgment of liberties granted by the Better Business Bureau.

C) ought to be expanded to include a ban on toy advertisements.

D) has a negligible effect on the health of the children who view advertisements.

17

Which choice provides the best evidence for the answer to the previous question?

A) Lines 46-49 ("McDonald's . . . meals")

B) Lines 63-64 ("Studies . . . children")

C) Lines 67-69 ("Rather . . . Bureau")

D) Lines 70-72 ("self-regulation . . . youth")

18

As used in line 68, "oversight" most nearly means

A) discovery.

B) inattention.

C) supervision.

D) omission.

19

Does the information presented in the graph provide evidence for the author's assertion that fast food ads have a detrimental effect on children's health?

A) Yes, because it indicates that children watch fast food ads more than they do any other type of ad.

B) Yes, because it proves that children frequently ask their parents for fast food items.

C) No, because it does nothing to address the effectiveness of the fast food ads included in the graph.

D) No, because it shows that most fast food restaurants actually run relatively few ads.

20

It can be inferred from the data in the chart that

A) children watch more fast food ads than adults do.

B) children under the age of six are highly susceptible to marketing tactics.

C) children are more often exposed to fast food ads than to other types of ads.

D) children under the age of six are exposed to a relatively large number of fast food ads.

21

For which restaurant listed in the graph is the number of ads viewed by 0-5 year-olds and 6-10 year-olds closest?

A) KFC

B) Burger King

C) Subway

D) McDonald's

CONTINUE

Questions 22-32 are based on the following passages.

The following two passages discuss the continued use of nuclear power in light of recent events in Fukushima, Japan. Passage 1 is adapted from a speech given by a nuclear energy lobbyist in 2012. Passage 2 is from a report written that same year by an independent research firm.

Passage 1

In recent years, the issue of global warming has become more and more pressing. Yet there has been frustratingly little agreement among policymakers regarding measures that would
Line actually tackle the problem. Fortunately, one of the best solutions
5 has been with us for decades; it has simply been overlooked. In order for this solution to be viable once more, however, it is necessary that we address climate policy with fresh eyes and with open minds. When it comes to clean, alternative energy, the fact remains that nuclear power is still one of the safest, most
10 effective options available.

It is understandable that, given the amount of negative press that nuclear power has suffered in recent years, advocating its use might strike some as a form of sacrilege. Indeed, it is impossible to talk about nuclear energy at all without
15 acknowledging the recent incident at Fukushima, in which an unusually large tsunami impacted four reactors at the Daiichi power plant. This accident made headlines all over the globe, sparking a host of alarmist theories regarding the hazardous release of radioactive materials. In reality, the amount of
20 radioactive material that escaped into the environment was insignificant. The Nuclear and Industrial Safety Agency (NISA) estimates that just 0.16% of the reactor's total inventory was released. Also, because reactor substances have very short half-lives, these materials were reduced to one sixteenth of
25 their original activity within a month of the incident. While the accident at Fukushima certainly substantiates the idea that new reactors should be built farther inland, there is no reason to assume—because of one aberrant gasp of nature—that nuclear power is unsafe. The reality is quite the opposite.
30 According to the World Nuclear Association, in over six decades of nuclear power, only three major accidents have ever occurred among the 435 nuclear power plants currently operational worldwide. And with advances in safety technology following Fukushima, the probability of future accidents
35 continues to decline. We should not allow a few problems to distract us from the tremendous benefits of nuclear power— namely, that it provides clean, affordable energy without emitting greenhouse gases. Nuclear power deserves both our reconsideration and our reinvestment.

Passage 2

40 Soon after its development in the 1950s and 1960s, nuclear power was hailed by many as the clean and safe energy alternative which we had long been seeking. The facts of history, however, have shown that these initial prognostications were both naïve and shortsighted. The two previous nuclear
45 meltdowns of Three Mile Island (1979) and Chernobyl (1986) notwithstanding, the most recent catastrophe at Fukushima, Japan should have forced even the most stalwart advocates of nuclear power to question their basic assumptions. Unfortunately, misinformation regarding the incident abounds,
50 largely due to questionable statistics indicating the amount of radioactive core material that was released into the atmosphere. No amount of math can change the fact that large quantities of cesium-137 were released into the air and sea on the day of the Fukushima disaster; despite the best cleanup efforts of the
55 Japanese government, it is impossible to say for certain what the full extent of radioactive contamination is, or will be, both for Japan and for the Pacific Ocean at large. While many would like to convince themselves that the disaster of Fukushima has now been relegated to the past, the fact remains that we will likely be
60 living with its effects for years, if not decades, to come.

As neuroscientist John C. Lilly once said regarding nuclear power, "We're playing around with something we don't know anything about. This is the stuff of stars, not of the planet." In defiance of all the evidence to the contrary, a small cadre of
65 die-hards continues to insist that nuclear power is a clean, cost-effective option—in fact, that it is the best alternative to fossil fuels that we currently have available. There is nothing clean about an environment so contaminated with radioactive waste that it is still uninhabitable two years later. Nor is there anything
70 cost-effective about $20 billion in taxpayer dollars—the cost-to-date of cleaning up after Fukushima. While it is a fact that our world requires new and alternative energy sources, the recent nuclear catastrophe at Fukushima provides indisputable evidence of a risky and unsafe technology.

22

The author of Passage 1 uses the word "alarmist" in line 18 in order to suggest that problems with nuclear power

A) are largely exaggerated.

B) require immediate action.

C) incite fear among scientists.

D) involve political propaganda.

CONTINUE

23

As used in line 3, "measures" most nearly means

A) examinations.

B) initiatives.

C) estimates.

D) comparisons.

24

The main purpose of Passage 1 is to

A) criticize the owners of the Daiichi power plant.

B) promote nuclear power as a source of energy.

C) raise awareness about global warming.

D) question the accuracy of current science journalism.

25

Which choice provides the best evidence for the answer to the previous question?

A) Lines 6-8 ("it is . . . minds")

B) Lines 8-10 ("When it . . . available")

C) Lines 12-13 ("advocating . . . sacrilege")

D) Lines 13-17 ("Indeed . . . plant")

26

How would the author of Passage 1 most likely respond to the comment in lines 63-66 ("In defiance . . . option") of Passage 2?

A) There is a large quantity of ambiguous evidence.

B) The facts clearly indicate that nuclear power is safe.

C) Most people agree that nuclear power is dangerous.

D) The need for energy overshadows the potential threat to the environment.

27

It can be inferred that the author of Passage 2 regards the Fukushima incident as

A) an addition to the list of nuclear disasters.

B) an event unlikely to cause future problems.

C) a reason to develop more efficient nuclear energy.

D) a misunderstood government investment.

28

Which choice provides the best evidence for the answer to the previous question?

A) Lines 41-42 ("nuclear . . . seeking")

B) Lines 46-48 ("the most recent . . . assumptions")

C) Lines 55-57 ("it is impossible . . . at large")

D) Lines 61-63 ("As neuroscientist . . . about")

29

Which best describes the relationship between Passage 1 and Passage 2?

A) Passage 1 agrees with the main line of reasoning behind Passage 2.

B) Passage 1 quotes a scientific study that is directly refuted by Passage 2.

C) Passage 2 presents a critical perspective on a situation viewed less pessimistically in Passage 1.

D) Passage 2 introduces new historical evidence that further develops the argument made in Passage 1.

30

The author of Passage 1 would most likely respond to the statement in lines 66-67 ("in fact . . . available") with

A) anxiety.

B) ambivalence.

C) animosity.

D) agreement.

31

As used in line 41, "hailed" most nearly means

A) invited.

B) welcomed.

C) honored.

D) introduced.

32

The final paragraph of Passage 2 functions primarily to

A) honor the ideas of neuroscientist John C. Lilly.

B) question the validity of recent studies of the benefits of nuclear power.

C) portray supporters of nuclear power as irresponsible.

D) encourage concerned citizens to take action.

CONTINUE ➡

Questions 33-42 are based on the following passage.

In the following excerpt from a 1917 speech, American social reformer Carrie Chapman Catt considers the then-heated issue of voting rights for women.

Woman suffrage is inevitable. Suffragists knew it before November 4, 1917; opponents afterward. Distinct causes made it inevitable.

Line
5   First, the history of our country. Ours is a nation born of revolution, of rebellion against a system of government so securely entrenched in the customs and traditions of human society that in 1776 it seemed impregnable. From the beginning of things, nations had been ruled by kings and for kings, while the people served and paid the cost. The American
10 Revolutionists boldly proclaimed the heresies: "Taxation without representation is tyranny." "Governments derive their just powers from the consent of the governed." The colonists won, and the nation which was established as a result of their victory has held unfailingly that these two fundamental principles of
15 democratic government are not only the spiritual source of our national existence but have been our chief historic pride and at all times the sheet anchor of our liberties.

Eighty years after the Revolution, Abraham Lincoln welded those two maxims into a new one: "Ours is a government of
20 the people, by the people, and for the people." Fifty years more passed and the president of the United States, Woodrow Wilson, in a mighty crisis of the nation, proclaimed to the world: "We are fighting for the things which we have always carried nearest to our hearts: for democracy, for the right of those who submit to
25 authority to have a voice in their own government."

All the way between these immortal aphorisms, political leaders have declared unabated faith in their truth. Not one American has arisen to question their logic in the 141 years of our national existence. However stupidly our country may have
30 evaded the logical application at times, it has never swerved from its devotion to the theory of democracy as expressed by those two axioms . . .

With such a history behind it, how can our nation escape the logic it has never failed to follow, when its last un-enfranchised
35 class calls for the vote? Behold our Uncle Sam floating the banner with one hand, "Taxation without representation is tyranny," and with the other seizing the billions of dollars paid in taxes by women to whom he refuses "representation." Behold him again, welcoming the boys of twenty-one and the newly
40 made immigrant citizen to "a voice in their own government" while he denies that fundamental right of democracy to thousands of women public school teachers from whom many of these men learn all they know of citizenship and patriotism, to women college presidents, to women who preach in our
45 pulpits, interpret law in our courts, preside over our hospitals, write books and magazines, and serve in every uplifting moral

and social enterprise. Is there a single man who can justify such inequality of treatment, such outrageous discrimination? Not one . . .

50   Second, the suffrage for women already established in the United States makes woman suffrage for the nation inevitable. When Elihu Root, as president of the American Society of International Law, at the eleventh annual meeting in Washington, April 26, 1917, said, "The world cannot be half democratic and
55 half autocratic. It must be all democratic or all Prussian. There can be no compromise," he voiced a general truth. Precisely the same intuition has already taught the blindest and most hostile foe of woman suffrage that our nation cannot long continue a condition under which government in half its territory rests upon
60 the consent of half of the people and in the other half upon the consent of all the people; a condition which grants representation to the taxed in half of its territory and denies it in the other half; a condition which permits women in some states to share in the election of the president, senators, and representatives and
65 denies them that privilege in others. It is too obvious to require demonstration that woman suffrage, now covering half our territory, will eventually be ordained in all the nation. No one will deny it. The only question left is when and how will it be completely established.

33

What is the speaker's main point about the founding principles of the United States?

A) Although they have been unevenly applied, they are still important to United States citizens.

B) Since they were responsible for revolution in the past, they will continue to cause political upheaval.

C) They are internationally popular, but untenable in practice.

D) While they are fundamentally flawed, they have secured the rights of United States citizens.

34

Which choice provides the best evidence for the answer to the previous question?

A) Lines 4-7 ("Ours is . . . impregnable")

B) Lines 18-20 ("Eighty years . . . the people")

C) Lines 29-32 ("However . . . two axioms")

D) Lines 52-56 ("When Elihu Root . . . truth")

CONTINUE

35

Catt mentions "the boys of twenty-one and the newly made immigrant citizen" (lines 39-40) as examples of

A) individuals who have thwarted women's efforts to gain suffrage.

B) people who are enfranchised under current American laws.

C) undeserving recipients of special treatment.

D) citizens who have always enjoyed the right to vote.

36

As used in line 41, "fundamental" most nearly means

A) basic.

B) theoretical.

C) easy.

D) supporting.

37

In this speech, Carrie Chapman Catt does which of the following to promote women's suffrage?

A) Discusses the future challenges that the United States will most likely face

B) Cites the international reputation of the United States

C) Alludes to the economic benefits of universal suffrage

D) Mentions specific women who have campaigned for the right to vote

38

Catt indicates that the eventual adoption of women's suffrage across the nation is

A) unprecedented.

B) precarious.

C) unwarranted.

D) inevitable.

39

Which choice provides the best evidence for the answer to the previous question?

A) Lines 7-9 ("From the . . . paid the cost")

B) Lines 26-27 ("All the way . . . their truth")

C) Lines 35-38 ("Behold our . . . representation")

D) Lines 65-67 ("It is . . . all the nation")

40

As used in line 63, "share in" most nearly means

A) distribute.

B) receive.

C) participate in.

D) endure.

41

Which choice best describes the structure of the passage?

A) A personal history is narrated, and that history is related to the speaker's main point.

B) A position is stated, and distinct reasons for that position are explained.

C) The attributes of the United States are systematically reviewed.

D) Certain principles are stated, and those principles are methodically debunked.

42

The stance that Catt takes in the passage is best described as that of

A) a well-informed advocate for women's rights.

B) a disillusioned citizen of a non-democratic nation.

C) an unbiased historian of United States politics.

D) an idealist who supports the status quo.

Questions 43-52 are based on the following passage and supplementary material.

This passage is adapted from the article "Insect Parasites and Their Deadly Adaptations" by Nathaniel Hunt.

"Nature red in tooth and claw," goes the old saying, and nature is indeed home to violence and bloodshed. Some creatures don't just kill their prey, however. The wasp
Line *Hymenoepimecis argyraphaga* parasitically takes control of its
5 prey, before using it to reproduce. This wasp, native to Costa Rica, has developed a novel predation strategy that is designed to help its larvae successfully construct cocoons. In something that would be at home in a science fiction film, this wasp is able to control the mind of the orb-weaving spider *Plesiometa*
10 *argyra*. This may well be the most extensive example of parasitic behavioral modification found among insects.

H. argyraphaga was first extensively studied by Dr. William G. Eberhard in 2000. Its larvae are capable of changing a spider's behavior, apparently through chemical
15 means. First, an adult wasp attacks an orb-weaving spider. If the wasp's sting is successful, the spider is left paralyzed. The adult wasp then deposits a larva onto the tip of the spider's abdomen. By the time the spider is able to regain movement, the adult wasp has left and the spider can resume its normal
20 behavior. The larva, for its part, remains clinging to the belly of the spider. It feeds off of the spider's juices, puncturing small holes in its carapace in order to suck out nourishment.

What happens next is truly horrifying. Somehow, the larva is able to influence the behavior of the spider. Exactly how the
25 larva is able to change the spider's behavior is unknown, but the larva makes the spider act in extremely specific ways. The

spider's normal five-step web-making pattern is reduced to only two steps. With three phases of its pattern suppressed, the spider creates abnormal, reinforced webs that are much smaller
30 than usual. These abnormal webs aren't designed to catch prey; rather, they are designed to support the wasp's cocoon. Once the spider is finished weaving this abnormal web, the larva kills it.

The stronger web strands serve to support the cocoon
35 in the event of rain, and the whole construction's elevated placement keeps it far from the dangerous ants that lurk in Costa Rica's forests. While it's currently unknown how the larva is able to control the spider to build a platform for itself, Eberhard hypothesizes that some sort of fast-acting chemical
40 is responsible. When he studied infected spiders in the lab, he found that they built the abnormal webs for several days before recovering. This implies that, regardless of how the wasp larva is controlling the spider, the behavior-altering effect lingers for quite some time. He further notes that it's been known for some
45 time that the behavior of orb-weaving spiders can be influenced through chemical means.

There are many cases of parasites influencing their hosts' behavior. For example, the microscopic *Toxoplasma gondii* can influence the behavior of rats, making them more susceptible to
50 being preyed upon by cats. A feline host is crucial to *T. gondii*'s life cycle, and infected rats display slower reaction time and a decreased fear of cat urine. However, *H. argyraphaga* is rare among behavior-altering parasites because of how specific and extensive the "mind-control" is. To put it simply, some
55 parasites can tweak a host's actions, but *H. argyraphaga* can change a host's manner of operating completely. As Eberhard notes, "It may be the most finely directed alteration of host behavior ever attributed to an insect parasitoid."

The Effects of *H. argyraphaga* on *Plesiometa argyra*

	Number of Steps Used in Web-Making Pattern			
	Non-Infected Spider	Infected Spider #1	Infected Spider #2	Infected Spider #3
Day 1	5	2	2	2
Day 2	5	2	2	2
Day 3	5	2	2	2
Day 4	5	5	2	2
Day 5	5	5	2	5
Day 6	5	5	5	5

CONTINUE

43

As used in line 6, "a novel" most nearly means

A) a strange.

B) an untested.

C) a revolutionary.

D) an experimental.

44

The passage indicates that *H. argyraphaga*'s parasitic behavior is

A) fully explained by a chemical mechanism.

B) admirable and worthy of further study.

C) unusual in its precision and scope.

D) closely paralleled by that of *T. gondii*.

45

Which choice provides the best evidence for the answer to the previous question?

A) Lines 23-24 ("Somehow . . . of the spider")

B) Lines 37-40 ("While it's . . . is responsible")

C) Lines 50-52 ("A feline host . . . of cat urine")

D) Lines 52-54 ("However . . . 'mind-control' is")

46

The author uses the phrase "science fiction" in line 8 to suggest that *H. argyraphaga*'s ability is

A) excessively violent.

B) exaggerated by researchers.

C) so unusual that it seems unreal.

D) still yet to be observed in nature.

47

In context, what is the primary function of the second and third paragraphs (lines 12-33)?

A) They detail a process that helps *Plesiometa argyra* reproduce successfully.

B) They outline the specific parasitic tactics used by *H. argyraphaga*.

C) They explain a complex biological phenomenon by using an analogy.

D) They lament the gruesome behavior that is necessary for survival in the wild.

48

As used in line 31, "support" most nearly means

A) defend.

B) hold up.

C) encourage.

D) subsidize.

49

In the fourth paragraph (lines 34-46), what does the author claim is still unknown?

A) How the larva attaches to the spider's carapace

B) How long the effects of the infection last

C) How the larva is capable of changing the spider's behavior

D) How the larva benefits from the spider

50

The author's main purpose in including the quote at the end of the passage (lines 57-58) is to

A) underscore the distinctiveness of *H. argyraphaga*'s parasitic behavior.

B) praise the effectiveness of *H. argyraphaga*'s survival adaptation.

C) suggest that insect parasites do not typically have advanced survival techniques.

D) confirm that *H. argyraphaga* is the most lethal parasite known to date.

51

Do the data in the table support the author's claim about how *H. argyraphaga* impacts the web-making of *Plesiometa argyra*?

A) Yes, because the infected spiders use an abnormal two-step pattern that is not exhibited by the non-infected spider.

B) Yes, because only the infected spiders are able to make a normal web in only two steps.

C) No, because not all of the spiders use the two-step web-making pattern mentioned by the author.

D) No, because for each given spider the web-making pattern returns to five steps.

52

Based on the table, is the effect of *H. argyraphaga* permanent or temporary, and which statement made by the author is most consistent with that data?

A) Permanent; "With three . . . than usual" (lines 28-30)

B) Permanent; "Once the . . . kills it" (lines 31-33)

C) Temporary; "When he . . . recovering" (lines 40-42)

D) Temporary; "He further . . . means" (lines 44-46)

STOP

If you finish before time is called, you may check your work on this section only.
Do not turn to any other section.

No Test Material On This Page

Answer Key: TEST 8

Test 8

PASSAGE 1
Fiction

1. C
2. B
3. D
4. B
5. C
6. D
7. C
8. A
9. A
10. B

PASSAGE 2
Social Science

11. D
12. C
13. D
14. C
15. D
16. A
17. D
18. C
19. C
20. D
21. A

PASSAGE 3
Natural Science 1

22. A
23. B
24. B
25. B
26. B
27. A
28. B
29. C
30. D
31. B
32. C

PASSAGE 4
Global Conversation

33. A
34. C
35. B
36. A
37. B
38. D
39. D
40. C
41. B
42. A

PASSAGE 5
Natural Science 2

43. A
44. C
45. D
46. C
47. B
48. B
49. C
50. A
51. A
52. C

Once you have determined how many questions
you answered correctly, consult the chart on Page 174
to determine your **SAT Reading Test score.**

Please visit **ies2400.com/answers** for answer explanations.

Post-Test Analysis

This post-test analysis is essential if you want to see an improvement on your next test. Possible reasons for errors on the five passages in this test are listed here. Place check marks next to the types of errors that pertain to you, or write your own types of errors in the blank spaces.

TIMING AND ACCURACY

◇ Spent too long reading individual passages
◇ Spent too long answering each question
◇ Spent too long on a few difficult questions
◇ Felt rushed and made silly mistakes or random errors
◇ Unable to work quickly using textual evidence and POE

Other: _____

APPROACHING THE PASSAGES AND QUESTIONS

◇ Unable to effectively grasp a passage's tone or style
◇ Unable to effectively grasp a passage's topic or stance
◇ Did not understand the context of line references
◇ Did not eliminate false answers using strong evidence
◇ Answered questions using first impressions instead of POE
◇ Answered questions without checking or inserting final answer
◇ Eliminated correct answer during POE
◇ Consistent trouble with Word in Context vocabulary
◇ Consistent trouble with Command of Evidence questions
◇ Consistent trouble with passage comparison questions

Other: _____

> **Use this form** to better analyze your performance. If you don't understand why you made errors, there is no way that you can correct them!

FICTION: # CORRECT_____ # WRONG _____ # OMITTED _____

◇ Could not grasp the roles and attitudes of major characters
◇ Could not grasp the significance of particular scenes or images
◇ Difficulty understanding the author's style and language
◇ Difficulty understanding the tone, theme, and structure of the passage as a whole

Other: _____

SOCIAL SCIENCE AND
GLOBAL CONVERSATION: # CORRECT_____ # WRONG _____ # OMITTED _____

◇ Unable to grasp the overall argument or thesis of an individual passage
◇ Unable to work effectively with the specific data or evidence in a passage
◇ Unable to respond effectively to tone, structure, and vocabulary
◇ Difficulty working with the graphics and graphic questions in a Social Science passage
◇ Difficulty understanding the logic or methodology of a Social Science passage
◇ Difficulty with the style and language of a Global Conversation passage
◇ Difficulty with the main historical and political concepts of a Global Conversation passage

Other: _____

NATURAL SCIENCE: # CORRECT_____ # WRONG _____ # OMITTED _____

◇ Unable to grasp the overall argument or thesis of an individual passage
◇ Unable to work effectively with the specific data or evidence in a passage
◇ Unable to respond effectively to tone, structure, and vocabulary
◇ Difficulty understanding the significance of the theories or experiments presented
◇ Difficulty working with the graphics and graphic questions

Other: _____

TEST 9

Reading Test

65 MINUTES, 52 QUESTIONS

Turn to Section 1 of your answer sheet to answer the questions in this section.

Each passage or pair of passages below is followed by a number of questions. After reading each passage or pair, choose the best answer to each question based on what is stated or implied in the passage or passages and in any accompanying graphics (such as a table or graph).

Questions 1-10 are based on the following passage.

This passage is from Jane Austen, *Mansfield Park*, originally published in 1814. In the following scene, a young girl named Fanny Price has been sent to live with her wealthy relatives, the Bertrams. Mrs. Norris, another relative, is a prominent figure in the Bertram household.

The little girl performed her long journey in safety; and at Northampton was met by Mrs. Norris, who thus regaled in the credit of being foremost to welcome her, and in the
Line importance of leading her in to the others, and recommending
5 her to their kindness.
　　Fanny Price was at this time just ten years old, and though there might not be much in her first appearance to captivate, there was, at least, nothing to disgust her relations. She was small of her age, with no glow of complexion, nor any other
10 striking beauty; exceedingly timid and shy, and shrinking from notice; but her air, though awkward, was not vulgar, her voice was sweet, and when she spoke her countenance was pretty. Sir Thomas and Lady Bertram received her very kindly, and Sir Thomas, seeing how much she needed encouragement,
15 tried to be all that was conciliating: but he had to work against a most untoward gravity of deportment; and Lady Bertram, without taking half so much trouble, or speaking one word where he spoke ten, by the mere aid of a good-humoured smile, became immediately the less awful character of the
20 two.
　　The young people were all at home, and sustained their share in the introduction very well, with much good humour, and no embarrassment, at least on the part of the sons, who, at seventeen and sixteen, and tall of their age, had all the
25 grandeur of men in the eyes of their little cousin. The two girls were more at a loss from being younger and in greater awe of their father, who addressed them on the occasion with rather an injudicious particularity. But they were too much used to company and praise to have anything like natural shyness, and
30 their confidence increasing from their cousin's total want of it, they were soon able to take a full survey of her face and her frock in easy indifference.
　　They were a remarkably fine family, the sons very well-looking, the daughters decidedly handsome, and all of
35 them well-grown and forward for their age, which produced as striking a difference between the cousins in person, as education had given to their address; no one would have supposed the girls so nearly of an age as they really were. There were in fact but two years between the youngest and
40 Fanny. Julia Bertram was only twelve, and Maria but a year older. The little visitor meanwhile was as unhappy as possible. Afraid of everybody, ashamed of herself, and longing for the home she had left, she knew not how to look up, and could scarcely speak to be heard, or without crying. Mrs. Norris
45 had been talking to her the whole way from Northampton of her wonderful good fortune, and the extraordinary degree of gratitude and good behaviour which it ought to produce, and her consciousness of misery was therefore increased by the idea of its being a wicked thing for her not to be happy. The
50 fatigue, too, of so long a journey, became soon no trifling evil. In vain were the well-meant condescensions of Sir Thomas, and all the officious prognostications of Mrs. Norris that she would be a good girl; in vain did Lady Bertram smile and make her sit on the sofa with herself and pug, and vain was even the
55 sight of a gooseberry tart towards giving her comfort; she could scarcely swallow two mouthfuls before tears interrupted her, and sleep seeming to be her likeliest friend, she was taken to finish her sorrows in bed.

CONTINUE

1

Which choice best summarizes the passage?

A) A young girl navigates the awkwardness of moving in with distant relatives

B) A young girl cringes at the idea of living with an unusually snobby and abusive family.

C) A young girl daydreams of a life of riches and contemplates her new role.

D) A young girl exhibits distress when she is assigned new responsibilities within a wealthy home.

2

The passage most clearly implies that Sir Thomas's attempts to interact with Fanny were

A) dishonest.

B) inspired.

C) futile.

D) upsetting.

3

Which choice provides the best evidence for the answer to the previous question?

A) Lines 13-15 ("Sir Thomas . . . conciliating")

B) Lines 15-16 ("but . . . deportment")

C) Lines 49-51 ("The fatigue . . . Sir Thomas")

D) Lines 55-58 ("She could . . . in bed")

4

As used in line 30, "want of" most nearly means

A) desire for.

B) search for.

C) fulfillment of.

D) lack of.

5

The descriptions of the family (lines 33-41) mainly serve to

A) provide insight into the motivations of a wealthy social group.

B) underscore why Fanny was both shy and intimidated.

C) juxtapose Fanny's education with that of her cousins.

D) explain and foreshadow an impending dispute.

6

As used in line 35, "forward" most nearly means

A) mature.

B) presumptuous.

C) progressive.

D) courageous

7

As presented in the passage, after meeting the family, Fanny is described as feeling

A) not only sad but also guilty about her feelings.

B) homesick and bitter despite her initial good spirits.

C) jealous of her cousins because of their beauty and personalities.

D) overwhelmed by the worldliness of her new companions.

CONTINUE

8

Which choice provides the best evidence for the answer to the previous question?

A) Line 41 ("The little . . . possible")

B) Lines 42-44 ("Afraid of . . . crying")

C) Lines 44-47 ("Mrs. Norris . . . produce")

D) Lines 47-49 ("and her . . . happy")

9

The narrator implies that Mrs. Norris

A) had ulterior motives when preparing Fanny to meet the family.

B) was not to be trusted due to her biased views of the family.

C) may have been so overzealous in her introductions that they had an adverse effect on Fanny.

D) was a strict disciplinarian and warned Fanny that she must be appreciative and well behaved.

10

As used in lines 57-58, "she was taken to finish her sorrows in bed" indicates that

A) since Fanny could not be consoled by food or kindness, sleep was the only option.

B) Fanny was sent to bed as a punishment for her tears.

C) Fanny was moved to another room so she could discuss her sadness in private.

D) everything would seem better to Fanny after a long night's sleep.

Questions 11-21 are based on the following passage.

"Free running" is a sport that involves racing on foot and overcoming obstacles in terrain. In this passage, the author explains the role of free running in the life of one contemporary young man.

The first time you meet Paolo, a spry twenty year-old, your impression may deceive you into thinking that he is just another youth emerging from his teenage years and living in one of Rio
Line de Janeiro's quickly-growing suburban communities. Jeans and
5 T-shirt and sneakers, a pierced ear and a few tattoos, a three-day stubble, and no trepidation about standing his ground when challenged, he enjoys clubbing with his friends. Sometimes, he stays up all night. He has his iPhone and he likes his music loud. With a cursory glance, you might well label him the kind
10 of person who makes the members of an older generation feel a little insecure and mutter to themselves that they don't know what today's youth is coming to.

A more perceptive eye would notice other things. There is a sense of controlled strength in the way he holds his body.
15 His movements are purposeful, lithe, and economic; these are movements that denote an athlete. When you chat with Paolo, he responds softly, yet firmly and precisely. His eyes look at you directly. They evaluate and consider intelligently, and when Paolo smiles, he does so with encompassing warmth. You realize
20 that you are talking to someone who has already known both difficult and blissful times and who is determined to use his varied knowledge of life in his future development. Paolo is clearly a young man who is going far—and not solely with the aid of his feet.

25 Paolo focuses his remarkable stores of energy on free running, an activity often confused with the sport of parkour. This is understandable since, on the surface at least, the two have similarities. Parkour came first: it is a sport that involves finding the fastest and most efficient way of getting from A to B, that
30 is, in a straight line with no deviation on account of the terrain. Sebastien Foucan, the world's foremost exponent of parkour, developed the sport from the ideas of his father, who had trained soldiers in the French army. Foucan's friend and rival, David Bell, developed free running, which some people call "fancy
35 parkour." For Bell, parkour's sole focus on speed and direction precluded opportunities for individual runners to express their own feelings and personalities. Each person's body has a certain individuality; thus, since there is often more than one way to overcome an obstacle, free running allows each runner to create
40 a highly personalized art of movement.

To the outsider, watching Paolo train is rather like watching a ballet dancer rehearse. Paolo himself would not take the description as far as that, but he does admit that break-dancing can be seen as a similar form of self-expression. He records
45 videos of his "rehearsals" and later adds music to them and

CONTINUE

puts them online, where they already boast a modest following. Okay, he agrees, some people call it "just showing off." But then he explains that "in a way, you could say the same thing about David Beckham," the famous athlete. "He's got style and
50 he knows it and he shows it. That's why he is who he is." Paolo knows that some people are wary of free running because it is dangerous and involves scaling walls and leaping from roofs, activities that bring to mind daredevils, rebels, even burglars. When questioned further, he shrugs and asks, "Why conform to
55 what society wants?"

Paolo knows what he wants: he wants to make a career of free running. He wants to be a stuntman. He knows that his path will not be easy, that his actions can be dangerous, that his luck has been plentiful so far—just a few sprained ankles and bruised
60 bones. He knows that there's a lot of competition, too, and a lot of red tape before he can make it into the profession. He knows that he has to give up some things in order to get what he wants: he had a girlfriend when he was thirteen but, in the end, they broke up because he spent more time on free running than on
65 her. Paolo also knows that, if he does succeed—and he will—he will have achieved his dream.

11

As used in line 15, "economic" most nearly means

A) mathematical.
B) lucrative.
C) practical.
D) logical.

12

The purpose of the second paragraph is to

A) highlight Paolo's amiable qualities.
B) describe the traits that helped Paolo become a respected athlete.
C) imply that Paolo comes from a relatively wealthy background.
D) show what an observant person would notice about Paolo.

13

As used in line 36, "precluded" most nearly means

A) ruled out.
B) expelled.
C) dismissed.
D) banned.

14

What does the author imply about parkour and free running?

A) Both parkour and free running involve finding the quickest route to a goal.
B) Both parkour and free running originated in France.
C) Free running offers more room for expression than parkour.
D) Free running is more often associated with rebellious activities than parkour.

15

Which choice provides the best evidence for the answer to the previous question?

A) Lines 27-28 ("This is . . . similarities")
B) Lines 39-40 ("free running . . . movement")
C) Lines 41-42 ("To the . . . rehearse")
D) Lines 54-55 ("When questioned . . . wants?")

16

The author mostly likely uses the simile in lines 41-42 to

A) suggest that Paolo could become a ballet dancer.
B) insinuate that Paolo has previous experience in ballet.
C) imply that free running appears to be artistic like ballet.
D) hint that Paolo resents being compared to a ballet dancer.

17

According to the passage, which choice best describes Paolo's attitude toward free running?

A) Paolo is confident that he can turn free running into a career.
B) Paolo is uncertain that free running will help him escape from Rio de Janeiro.
C) Paolo regrets that free running required sacrificing his personal life.
D) Paolo is enthusiastic about free running but unaware of its history.

18

Which choice provides the best evidence for the answer to the previous question?

A) Lines 13-14 ("There is . . . body")

B) Lines 25-26 ("Paolo . . . parkour")

C) Lines 44-46 ("He records . . . online")

D) Lines 65-66 ("Paolo . . . dream")

19

The author uses the phrase "so far" in line 59 to suggest that

A) Paolo may experience more serious injuries in the future.

B) Paolo invites bad luck by pursuing free running.

C) Paolo attributes his success to extraordinary luck.

D) Paolo will never become a stuntman.

20

The author's attitude towards Paolo is best described as one of

A) admiration.

B) astonishment.

C) ambivalence.

D) admonition.

21

Which of the following best describes the developmental pattern of the passage?

A) A humorous character portrait, followed by strong criticisms of the individual introduced earlier

B) An overview of personal obstacles, followed by a discussion of the measures necessary for overcoming those obstacles

C) Commentary on the difference between appearance and reality, followed by a systematic condemnation of conformity

D) Impressions of an individual, followed by a discussion of multiple aspects of a single activity

Questions 22-32 are based on the following passage and supplementary material.

This passage is adapted from A.F. Thomasin, "'I Am Not a Dolphin, I Am a Human Being!': Evaluating Dolphin Personhood."

Dolphins have long been considered one of the smartest animal species on Earth. During decades of research, scientists have estimated that dolphins are the second most intelligent
Line species on the planet, ranking only behind humans. This high
5 degree of intelligence has recently led to calls for greater legal protections for dolphins and whales. In 2012, scientists called for a change in how cetaceans are treated, dubbing these creatures "non-human persons." The Indian government responded in 2013 with a law that defines dolphins as such, and
10 that bans keeping them in captivity.

Just how smart are dolphins? Bottlenose dolphin possess brains that are larger overall than those of humans, though they are smaller proportionally (i.e., they take up a smaller percentage of body weight). Dolphins are excellent problem-
15 solvers and are highly social, even clever. In one famous instance, a dolphin named Kelly managed to trick her trainers into giving her extra treats. She was rewarded each time she gave them a piece of trash she found in her enclosure. One day, she hid a paper bag under a rock, tearing off small pieces one at
20 a time and getting a new reward for each piece.

Dolphins are also very adaptable animals, capable of learning—and in some cases even of teaching. There have been documented cases of pods of dolphins developing a "culture," as demonstrated by one pod off the coast of Florida that has
25 contrived a novel way to catch fish. The dolphin pod splits into two groups. The dolphins in one group beat their tails against the ocean floor, driving up mud and silt. Fish are confused when they see this wall of mud, thinking that they've run into a solid barrier. When the fish swim over the "barrier," they fall
30 right into the waiting mouths of the other half of the pod. This dolphin behavior is displayed in only this one pod of dolphins, passed down for generations.

Finally—and most crucially—dolphins display self-awareness. When placed in front of mirrors, dolphins can
35 actually recognize themselves, something that most animals cannot do. "Individuality, consciousness, and self-awareness are no longer unique human properties," says Tom White, director of the Centre for Ethics and Business at Loyola Marymount University in Los Angeles.
40 Experts claim that dolphins are intelligent enough to warrant the same moral and ethical considerations that are granted to humans. Thus, biologists and specialists in animal behavior have joined with philosophers to call for treating dolphins as "non-human persons." Under these terms, killing
45 a dolphin would be tantamount to murder. Capturing and keeping one in captivity would be equal to kidnapping and

forced imprisonment. As it stands, dolphins do not have legal rights anywhere but India. Under international law, and many national laws, it is legal to trap, hunt, or capture dolphins;
50 commercial fishers still use harmful fishing methods that kill thousands of whales and dolphins each year.

In response to these new discoveries, and to the rising rates of dolphin killings, a group of scientists drafted a statement. At the 2012 meeting of the American Association
55 for the Advancement of Science, researchers released a Declaration of Rights for Cetaceans, advocating the establishment of legal rights for dolphins and whales.

Yet India's landmark ruling in 2013 may do little to change things overall. Since it has taken effect, dolphins have
60 continued to be hunted and killed elsewhere in the world. Other dolphins remain in captivity, in enclosures much smaller than their habitual ranges in the wild—in some cases, less than 1% in area. More research needs to be done and more action may well need to be taken, but it's tempting to imagine
65 the possibility of creating a closer bond to the second most intelligent animal on the planet.

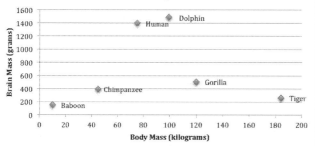

Brain to Body Mass Ratio in Various Species

22

The main purpose of the passage is to

A) advocate for certain rights.

B) counter experts' assertions.

C) answer a difficult question.

D) examine the implications of an assertion.

23

The primary purpose of the anecdote about Kelly the dolphin is to

A) provide evidence in to support a characterization.

B) transition from one topic to another.

C) engage the reader with an amusing aside.

D) question the veracity of a claim.

24

The truth of the claim in lines 34-36 ("When . . . do") relies on the assumption that

A) dolphins greatly enjoy looking in mirrors.

B) dolphins are the only non-human animals that can recognize their own reflections.

C) scientists are able to understand what a dolphin is thinking when it looks in the mirror.

D) there exists a reliable way in which to determine whether dolphins can recognize their own likenesses.

25

The passage indicates that

A) dolphins have expressed a wish for increased legal representation.

B) some people have made attempts to establish rights for dolphins.

C) dolphins have been known to trick both humans and other cetaceans.

D) society should more seriously consider granting increased rights to all animals.

26

Which choice provides the best evidence for the answer to the previous question?

A) Lines 15-17 ("In one . . . treats")

B) Lines 40-42 ("Experts . . . humans")

C) Lines 54-57 ("At the . . . whales")

D) Lines 61-63 ("Other . . . area")

27

The author's attitude toward the notion that dolphins should be granted legal rights based on their intelligence can be best described as

A) unreserved opposition.

B) healthy skepticism.

C) tempered engagement.

D) staunch support.

149

28

Which choice provides the best evidence for the answer to the previous question?

A) Lines 6-8 ("In 2012 . . . persons)

B) Lines 45-47 ("Capturing . . . imprisonment")

C) Lines 58-59 ("Yet . . . overall")

D) Lines 63-66 ("More . . . planet")

29

As used in line 44, "terms" most nearly means

A) expressions.

B) periods.

C) stipulations.

D) descriptions.

30

The information in the graph indicates that

A) gorillas have a higher body mass than tigers.

B) gorillas have a higher brain mass than humans.

C) gorillas have a lower brain mass than chimpanzees.

D) gorillas have a higher body mass than chimpanzees.

31

Both the passage and the data in the graph support which assertion?

A) A higher brain mass correlates to a higher intelligence.

B) A lower body mass correlates to a lower intelligence.

C) A lower brain to body mass ratio correlates to a higher intelligence.

D) A higher brain to body mass ratio correlates to a higher intelligence.

32

Based on the information in the chart, which two species have the most similar brain masses?

A) Baboons and Chimpanzees

B) Chimpanzees and Gorillas

C) Humans and Dolphins

D) Gorillas and Tigers

CONTINUE

Questions 33-42 are based on the following passages.

The first passage is adapted from the remarks upon signing the Civil Rights Act (1964) delivered by President Lyndon B. Johnson. The second passage is adapted from the address at the dedication of the Martin Luther King Memorial (2011) delivered by President Barack Obama.

Passage 1

We must not approach the observance and enforcement of this law in a vengeful spirit. Its purpose is not to punish. Its purpose is not to divide, but to end divisions—divisions which
Line have all lasted too long. Its purpose is national, not regional.
5   Its purpose is to promote a more abiding commitment to freedom, a more constant pursuit of justice, and a deeper respect for human dignity.

We will achieve these goals because most Americans are law-abiding citizens who want to do what is right.
10   This is why the Civil Rights Act relies first on voluntary compliance, then on the efforts of local communities and States to secure the rights of citizens. It provides for the national authority to step in only when others cannot or will not do the job.
15   This Civil Rights Act is a challenge to all of us to go to work in our communities and our States, in our homes and in our hearts, to eliminate the last vestiges of injustice in our beloved country.

So tonight I urge every public official, every religious
20 leader, every business and professional man, every workingman, every housewife—I urge every American—to join in this effort to bring justice and hope to all our people—and to bring peace to our land.

My fellow citizens, we have come now to a time of testing.
25 We must not fail.

Let us close the springs of racial poison. Let us pray for wise and understanding hearts. Let us lay aside irrelevant differences and make our Nation whole.

Passage 2

It is right for us to celebrate Dr. King's marvelous oratory,
30 but it is worth remembering that progress did not come from words alone. Progress was hard. Progress was purchased through enduring the smack of billy clubs and the blast of fire hoses. It was bought with days in jail cells and nights of bomb threats. For every victory during the height of the Civil Rights
35 Movement, there were setbacks and there were defeats.

We forget now, but during his life, Dr. King wasn't always considered a unifying figure. Even after rising to prominence, even after winning the Nobel Peace Prize, Dr. King was vilified by many, denounced as a rabble rouser and an agitator,
40 a communist and a radical. He was even attacked by his own people, by those who felt he was going too fast or those who felt he was going too slow; by those who felt he shouldn't meddle in issues like the Vietnam War or the rights of union workers. We know from his own testimony the doubts and the
45 pain this caused him, and that the controversy that would swirl around his actions would last until the fateful day he died.

Nearly 50 years after the March on Washington, our work, Dr. King's work, is not yet complete. We gather here at a moment of great challenge and great change. In the first
50 decade of this new century, we have been tested by war and by tragedy; by an economic crisis and its aftermath that has left millions out of work, and poverty on the rise, and millions more just struggling to get by. Indeed, even before this crisis struck, we had endured a decade of rising inequality and
55 stagnant wages. In too many troubled neighborhoods across the country, the conditions of our poorest citizens appear little changed from what existed 50 years ago—neighborhoods with underfunded schools and broken-down slums, inadequate health care, constant violence, neighborhoods in which too
60 many young people grow up with little hope and few prospects for the future.

Our work is not done. And so on this day, in which we celebrate a man and a movement that did so much for this country, let us draw strength from those earlier struggles.
65 First and foremost, let us remember that change has never been quick. Change has never been simple, or without controversy. Change depends on persistence. Change requires determination. It took a full decade before the moral guidance of Brown v. Board of Education was translated into the
70 enforcement measures of the Civil Rights Act and the Voting Rights Act, but those 10 long years did not lead Dr. King to give up. He kept on pushing, he kept on speaking, he kept on marching until change finally came.

33

The author of Passage 1 believes that freedom, justice, and human dignity for all is possible because

A) the majority of Americans are morally good and follow the law.

B) these ideals will be rigorously maintained by strict law enforcement.

C) political leaders can serve as exemplars of dignity and respect.

D) the obstacles to these goals have been entirely eliminated.

34

Which choice provides the best evidence for the answer to the previous question?

A) Lines 1-2 ("We . . . spirit")

B) Lines 8-9 ("We . . . right")

C) Lines 19-23 ("So . . . land")

D) Lines 26-28 ("Let . . . whole")

35

As used in line 12, "secure" most nearly means

A) attach.

B) seal.

C) protect.

D) obtain.

36

According to the author of Passage 2, the "time of testing" (line 24, Passage 1) is

A) an ongoing condition facing Americans.

B) a phrase used merely for rhetorical effect.

C) now primarily centered on international relations.

D) restricted to Dr. King's social activism.

37

Which choice provides the best evidence for the answer to the previous question?

A) Lines 29-31 ("It is . . . alone")

B) Lines 40-44 ("He was . . . workers")

C) Lines 47-49 ("Nearly . . . change")

D) Lines 68-72 ("It took . . . give up")

38

As used in line 55, "troubled" most nearly means

A) agitated.

B) perplexed.

C) bothered.

D) disadvantaged.

39

Which best describes the overall relationship between Passage 1 and Passage 2?

A) Passage 2 offers an evenhanded description of a situation that Passage 1 views as purely problematic.

B) Passage 2 restates in a different context the message presented in Passage 1.

C) Passage 2 emphasizes the negative effects of a development that Passage 1 treats in a positive fashion.

D) Passage 2 provides evidence that suggests that the argument in Passage 1 is based on flawed assumptions.

40

The author of Passage 1 would view the problems listed in Passage 2, lines 57-61 ("neighborhoods . . . future") as

A) evidence of the need for citizens, states, and the nation as a whole to work together to improve conditions.

B) examples of conditions that will not improve unless the national government takes decisive and sweeping action.

C) justification for state law enforcement to punish individuals who do not abide by the law.

D) insufficient to prove that racial injustice is a continuing problem.

41

Both authors would most likely agree with which of the following about any societal change?

A) It is easier to achieve than most Americans believe.

B) It requires the efforts of educated leaders.

C) It is especially challenging to accomplish when divisions are based on race.

D) It will be difficult to achieve without unity or resolve.

42

In the concluding paragraph of each passage, each author

A) qualifies his arguments with counter-evidence.

B) urges Americans to collectively bring about change in society.

C) shows what will happen to democratic values if Americans do not work together.

D) enlarges his apparent audience by addressing the global population.

CONTINUE

Questions 43-52 are based on the following passage and supplementary material.

This passage originally appeared as the article "Recent Research Puts a New 'Spin' on Water Molecules" by Cynthia Helzner.

The structure of an atom can be compared to the structure of a peach: the positively-charged protons and the uncharged neutrons are found in the center or nucleus (the peach pit),
Line while the negatively charged electrons orbit in the outer layers
5 (the edible fruit) of the peach. The analogy ends, though, when atoms combine. (Have you ever seen a peach with two pits?) By sharing electrons, individual atoms bond together to form molecules. Water, after all, is written as H2O because two hydrogen atoms (H) and one oxygen atom (O) bond together to
10 form a water molecule.

Each hydrogen nucleus contains one proton, and so one water molecule contains two hydrogen protons. Each of these protons spins in one of two directions: as a result, the two protons can either spin in the same direction or in opposite
15 directions.

If the protons spin in the same direction, the water is called ortho-water; if the protons spin in opposite directions, the water is called para-water. An isomer is a version of a molecule, and so ortho-water and para-water are referred to as nuclear spin
20 isomers of water. The para nuclear spin isomer is lower in energy than the ortho isomer is. Molecules tend to convert to their lowest-energy state, and so ortho-water tends to convert to para-water.

Scientists interested in studying the nuclear spin isomers
25 of water have found it difficult to do so because nuclear spin experiments are carried out at cryogenic (extremely cold) temperatures, at which water freezes. When frozen, water molecules do not move freely. This lack of free movement is problematic for researchers because free rotation is needed in
30 the study of the conversion of ortho-water to para-water.

Dr. Benno Meier and his research team devised an ingenious solution to the problem of water molecules sticking together: they enclosed individual water molecules in carbon buckyballs. Buckyballs are microscopic "cages" shaped like
35 hollow soccer balls. By encapsulating each water molecule within a buckyball, the researchers prevented the water molecules from sticking to each other and thereby kept the water from freezing, even though Meier's experiment was carried out at the below-freezing temperature of 5 Kelvin
40 (equivalent to -268°C, or approximately -450°F). Thus, the water molecules could rotate freely.

Next, the researchers had to figure out a way to measure the conversion of ortho-water to para-water. Individual proton spins are too small to see, even with the most powerful
45 microscopes, and so the scientists had to observe the water's

nuclear spin in an indirect way. They chose to track the water's bulk dielectric constant* as a measure of the ortho-to-para conversion process.

The results of Meier's experiment show that the bulk
50 dielectric constant of water decreases during the conversion of ortho-water to para-water. Dr. Meier explained that the bulk dielectric constant of water "depends on the spin isomer composition of the encapsulated water molecules." In other words, ortho-water has a different amount of polarization
55 than para-water. Thus, the decrease in water's bulk dielectric constant during the ortho-to-para conversion shows that water becomes less polar as ortho-water becomes para-water.

The ability to study the spin isomers of water has both theoretical and practical importance. Spin isomers are
60 significant across a wide array of scientific fields, including astrophysics, quantum theory (a model of how atoms and energy behave), and NMR (a process commonly used by chemists to deduce molecular structure). Gil Alexandrowicz, a nuclear spin isomer researcher, believes that understanding the
65 spin isomers of water could improve NMR signal resolution by a multiple of up to 100,000. "I believe that such experiments are possible and in fact our group is currently working towards that goal," said Alexandrowicz.

*Because the electrons shared between hydrogen and oxygen are not shared evenly, water is classified as a polar molecule. The degree of polarization of a molecule is measured by its dielectric constant. Similarly, the degree of polarization of an entire substance is measured by its bulk dielectric constant.

43

It can be inferred that the author views the analogy of a peach in the first paragraph as

A) completely apt and without drawbacks.

B) somewhat helpful but imperfect.

C) absolutely unrealistic and idealistic.

D) common among contemporary researchers.

44

As used in line 29, "rotation" most nearly means

A) exercise.

B) revolution.

C) sequence.

D) examination.

Shifting Dielectric Constants of H_2O as Ortho-H_2O changes to Para-H_2O

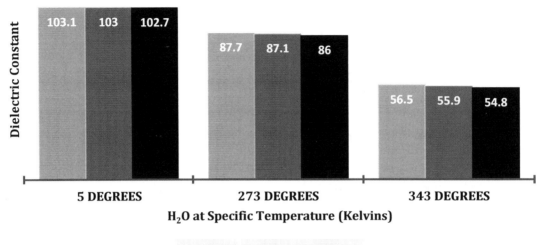

45

The passage indicates that Dr. Meier used dielectric constant as an indicator of water's nuclear spin because

A) water freezes at the cryogenic temperatures needed to observe nuclear spin.

B) the water molecule's nuclear spin is not directly observable.

C) the para isomer is lower in energy than the ortho isomer.

D) using carbon buckyballs proved too difficult and unhelpful.

46

Which choice provides the best evidence for the answer to the previous question?

A) Lines 7-8 ("By sharing . . . molecules")

B) Lines 16-18 ("If the protons . . . para-water")

C) Lines 43-46 ("Individual . . . way")

D) Lines 58-59 ("The ability . . . importance")

47

The author implies that Dr. Meier's solution was "ingenious" (line 32) because

A) it modified the physical properties of water, making it possible to conduct a hitherto challenging experiment.

B) it allowed scientists to change the number of hydrogen atoms in water molecules.

C) up until that point, it was considered impossible to study nuclear spin in water molecules.

D) it made it possible to see individual proton spins, which scientists could not see before.

48

Which choice provides the best evidence for the answer to the previous question?

A) Lines 24-27 ("Scientists . . . freezes")

B) Lines 35-41 ("By encapsulating . . . freely")

C) Lines 46-48 ("They chose . . . process")

D) Lines 66-68 ("I believe . . . Alexandrowicz")

49

As used in line 46, "track" most nearly means

A) pursue.

B) chase.

C) assign.

D) record.

50

Taken together, the data presented in the graph and the information in the passage best support which of the following statements?

A) It can be inferred that water predictably shifts in molecule composition from ortho-water to para-water.

B) The dielectric constant of water is solely dependent on temperature.

C) As time progresses, it can be inferred that more ortho-water is appearing.

D) Various substances have dielectric constants that depend on both temperature and time.

51

The author would most likely attribute the drop in dielectric constant for water at 5 Kelvin as represented in the graph to

A) the number of hydrogen atoms and oxygen atoms that bond together to form water.

B) the carbon buckyballs used to encapsulate water molecules.

C) the tendency of water molecules to convert from ortho-water to para-water.

D) the difficulty of measuring the free rotation of frozen water molecules.

52

The author of the passage would most likely consider the information in the graph to be

A) corroborated by Dr. Meier's experiment.

B) counterintuitive in light of the anticipated results.

C) unsubstantiated by any experiment conducted to date.

D) contradictory to trends in the dielectric constants of water.

STOP

If you finish before time is called, you may check your work on this section only.

Do not turn to any other section.

Answer Key: TEST 9

Test 9

PASSAGE 1
Fiction

1.   A
2.   C
3.   C
4.   D
5.   B
6.   A
7.   A
8.   D
9.   C
10. A

PASSAGE 2
Social Science

11. C
12. D
13. A
14. C
15. B
16. C
17. A
18. D
19. A
20. A
21. D

PASSAGE 3
Natural Science 1

22. D
23. A
24. D
25. B
26. C
27. C
28. D
29. C
30. D
31. D
32. C

PASSAGE 4
Global Conversation

33. A
34. B
35. C
36. A
37. C
38. D
39. B
40. A
41. D
42. B

PASSAGE 5
Natural Science 2

43. B
44. B
45. B
46. C
47. A
48. B
49. D
50. A
51. C
52. A

Once you have determined how many questions
you answered correctly, consult the chart on Page 174
to determine your **SAT Reading Test score.**

Please visit **ies2400.com/answers** for answer explanations.

Post-Test Analysis

This post-test analysis is essential if you want to see an improvement on your next test. Possible reasons for errors on the five passages in this test are listed here. Place check marks next to the types of errors that pertain to you, or write your own types of errors in the blank spaces.

TIMING AND ACCURACY

◇ Spent too long reading individual passages
◇ Spent too long answering each question
◇ Spent too long on a few difficult questions
◇ Felt rushed and made silly mistakes or random errors
◇ Unable to work quickly using textual evidence and POE
Other: _____

APPROACHING THE PASSAGES AND QUESTIONS

◇ Unable to effectively grasp a passage's tone or style
◇ Unable to effectively grasp a passage's topic or stance
◇ Did not understand the context of line references
◇ Did not eliminate false answers using strong evidence
◇ Answered questions using first impressions instead of POE
◇ Answered questions without checking or inserting final answer
◇ Eliminated correct answer during POE
◇ Consistent trouble with Word in Context vocabulary
◇ Consistent trouble with Command of Evidence questions
◇ Consistent trouble with passage comparison questions
Other: _____

> **Use this form** to better analyze your performance. If you don't understand why you made errors, there is no way that you can correct them!

FICTION: # CORRECT_____   # WRONG _____   # OMITTED _____

◇ Could not grasp the roles and attitudes of major characters
◇ Could not grasp the significance of particular scenes or images
◇ Difficulty understanding the author's style and language
◇ Difficulty understanding the tone, theme, and structure of the passage as a whole
Other: _____

SOCIAL SCIENCE AND
GLOBAL CONVERSATION: # CORRECT_____   # WRONG _____   # OMITTED _____

◇ Unable to grasp the overall argument or thesis of an individual passage
◇ Unable to work effectively with the specific data or evidence in a passage
◇ Unable to respond effectively to tone, structure, and vocabulary
◇ Difficulty working with the graphics and graphic questions in a Social Science passage
◇ Difficulty understanding the logic or methodology of a Social Science passage
◇ Difficulty with the style and language of a Global Conversation passage
◇ Difficulty with the main historical and political concepts of a Global Conversation passage
Other: _____

NATURAL SCIENCE: # CORRECT_____   # WRONG _____   # OMITTED _____

◇ Unable to grasp the overall argument or thesis of an individual passage
◇ Unable to work effectively with the specific data or evidence in a passage
◇ Unable to respond effectively to tone, structure, and vocabulary
◇ Difficulty understanding the significance of the theories or experiments presented
◇ Difficulty working with the graphics and graphic questions
Other: _____

TEST 10

Reading Test
65 MINUTES, 52 QUESTIONS

Turn to Section 1 of your answer sheet to answer the questions in this section.

Questions 1-10 are based on the following passage.

This passage is from Virginia Woolf, "Kew Gardens," originally published in 1919. Kew is the location of the Royal Botanic Gardens of the United Kingdom.

From the oval-shaped flower-bed there rose perhaps a hundred stalks spreading into heart-shaped or tongue-shaped leaves half way up and unfurling at the tip red or blue or
Line
5 yellow petals marked with spots of colour raised upon the surface; and from the red, blue or yellow gloom of the throat emerged a straight bar, rough with gold dust and slightly clubbed at the end. The petals were voluminous enough to be stirred by the summer breeze, and when they moved, the red, blue and yellow lights passed one over the other,
10 staining an inch of the brown earth beneath with a spot of the most intricate colour. The light fell either upon the smooth, grey back of a pebble, or the shell of a snail with its brown, circular veins, or falling into a raindrop, it expanded with such intensity of red, blue and yellow the thin walls of water
15 that one expected them to burst and disappear. Instead, the drop was left in a second silver grey once more, and the light now settled upon the flesh of a leaf, revealing the branching thread of fibre beneath the surface, and again it moved on and spread its illumination in the vast green spaces beneath the
20 dome of the heart-shaped and tongue-shaped leaves. Then the breeze stirred rather more briskly overhead and the colour was flashed into the air above, into the eyes of the men and women who walk in Kew Gardens in July.
The figures of these men and women straggled past the
25 flower-bed with a curiously irregular movement not unlike that of the white and blue butterflies who crossed the turf in zig-zag flights from bed to bed. The man was about six inches in front of the woman, strolling carelessly, while she bore on

with greater purpose, only turning her head now and then to
30 see that the children were not too far behind. The man kept this distance in front of the woman purposely, though perhaps unconsciously, for he wished to go on with his thoughts.
"Fifteen years ago I came here with Lily," he thought. "We sat somewhere over there by a lake and I begged her to
35 marry me all through the hot afternoon. How the dragonfly kept circling round us: how clearly I see the dragonfly and her shoe with the square silver buckle at the toe. All the time I spoke I saw her shoe and when it moved impatiently I knew without looking up what she was going to say: the whole of
40 her seemed to be in her shoe. And my love, my desire, were in the dragonfly; for some reason I thought that if it settled there, on that leaf, the broad one with the red flower in the middle of it, if the dragonfly settled on the leaf she would say "Yes" at once. But the dragonfly went round and round: it never
45 settled anywhere—of course not, happily not, or I shouldn't be walking here with Eleanor and the children—Tell me, Eleanor. D'you ever think of the past?"
"Why do you ask, Simon?"
"Because I've been thinking of the past. I've been thinking
50 of Lily, the woman I might have married. . . . Well, why are you silent? Do you mind my thinking of the past?"
"Why should I mind, Simon? Doesn't one always think of the past, in a garden with men and women lying under the trees? Aren't they one's past, all that remains of it, those
55 men and women, those ghosts lying under the trees, . . . one's happiness, one's reality?"
"For me, a square silver shoe buckle and a dragonfly—"

CONTINUE

Test 10

1

Which choice best describes what happens in the passage?

A) A man takes a solitary stroll through a garden.

B) A man ignores the nature around him and becomes lost in his thoughts.

C) A man is prompted by his surroundings to recall moments from his past.

D) A man expresses his marital unhappiness to his spouse.

2

Which choice best describes the developmental pattern of the passage?

A) A story about a specific location becomes an ode to nature.

B) An ongoing argument is recalled by two characters.

C) A specific example about love and loss facilitates a discussion of local scenery.

D) A scenic description gives way to a specific discussion.

3

As used in line 7, "clubbed" most nearly means

A) battered.

B) stunned.

C) hobbled.

D) thickened.

4

As used in line 10, "staining" most nearly means

A) tainting.

B) obfuscating.

C) influencing.

D) illuminating.

5

The main purpose of the second paragraph is to

A) provide an assessment of the story's setting.

B) explain the relationship between Lily and Simon.

C) describe the physical appearances of the people who regularly visit Kew Gardens.

D) introduce the vignette's main characters.

6

In the passage, the dragonfly serves to

A) indicate that Lily did not reciprocate the man's feelings.

B) suggest that creatures in the park are engaged in its visitors' personal lives.

C) display the man's somewhat frantic demeanor during his proposal to Lily.

D) provide imagery to show how the gardens were once arranged.

7

Which choice provides the best evidence for the answer to the previous question?

A) Lines 35-37 ("How the dragonfly . . . toe")

B) Lines 41-45 ("for some . . . anywhere")

C) Lines 46-47 ("Tell me . . . the past?")

D) Lines 49-50 ("Because . . . married")

8

In his present emotional state, Simon is best described as

A) anxious over unresolved matters.

B) simultaneously ecstatic and disgruntled by everyday problems.

C) nostalgic despite his general appearance of contentment.

D) embittered because of past rejection.

9

Which choice provides the best evidence for the answer to the previous question?

A) Lines 11-15 ("The light . . . disappear")

B) Lines 24-27 ("The figures . . . bed")

C) Lines 30-32 ("The man . . . thoughts")

D) Lines 37-39 ("All the time . . . say")

10

It can most reasonably be inferred that the author sees the scenery in Kew Gardens as

A) incidental.

B) affecting.

C) enervating.

D) agitating.

CONTINUE

Questions 11-21 are based on the following passages.

In the passages that follow, two authors consider new technology and how its development has shaped modern society.

Passage 1

Can you imagine going a full day without using technology? Few of us can; in fact, take away our cell phones for a couple of hours, and most of us will begin to feel
Line something like existential panic. In ways that we immediately
5 recognize, and in a few ways that we don't, technology commands the ways we communicate, the ways we gather information, even the ways we prepare our food.

The devices responsible—in the above cases, the cell phone, computer, and microwave—are just a few of the
10 technologies that have been invented over the past 40 years. Often, it has taken a while for these inventions to catch on. The first cell phone call was placed on April 3, 1973; however, cell phones did not become mainstream until 2003. Personal computers were also created in the 1970s, but did not command
15 a mass market until the early 1990s. Amazingly, while microwave ovens were first available to the public in the mid-1950s, it was not until the late 1970s that they became widely used.

Each of these pieces of technology has been successfully
20 marketed in the same way: this product will help you meet your needs, make your life easier, and—best of all—save you time! In fact, we do have more leisure time than those in past generations, at least according to the Boston Federal Reserve. In a recent study, this institution found that since 1963, "leisure
25 time for men increased by 6-8 hours per week and for women by 4-8 hours per week." Yet today, people regularly claim to be busy to the point of exhaustion. And according to sociology professor Judy Wacjman, technology itself may be responsible for this burnout effect. To quote Wacjman: "Technological
30 utopians once dreamt of the post-industrial society as one of leisure. Instead, we are more like characters in *Alice in Wonderland*, running ever faster and faster to stand still."

Technology, it seems, is both a handmaiden and a temptress. While working hours may have decreased, the
35 temptation to accomplish more work, or to go all-out finding new leisure pursuits, has been turbocharged. After all, utilize the right technology and you can have it all, or so we're told.

Passage 2

For the past five years, I have taught a university course that meets twice a week and that considers the psychological
40 and ethical aspects of modern marketing practices. To gauge the psychology of my students, I always begin the semester with a veiled experiment—nothing unethical, though.

In the first class of the first week, I assign my students an article on the evils of modern technology: "The Flight
45 from Conversation" by Sherry Turkle, a condemnation of the conversation-killing, dumbing-down effects of texting and social media, is always reliable. The students read, absorb, and are repulsed. They chime in with their own experiences of the inanity of technology—websites that include "ClownDating"
50 and "Pictures of Hipsters Taking Pictures of Food," tone-deaf singing routines that somehow acquire 35 million views on YouTube, text messages without a single correctly-spelled word—and leave class devilishly amused at the prospect that society is falling apart.

55 However, next class, I switch gears and offer up an article that hails all the benefits technology imparts: the optimistic "Mind Over Mass Media" by Steven Pinker is my stalwart here. The students read, absorb, and this time laud the databases, the e-mails, the education platforms, the new and
60 rapidly-delivered forms of entertainment that have enhanced their lives.

While I have never been surprised that my students have an ambivalent relationship to technology, I am surprised that such ambivalence has not waned. You would think they'd
65 be used to all this by now. Instead, the strength of that love-hate push-and-pull only grows stronger with each passing semester. With the growth of technology has come the growth of a psychodrama that involves increasingly high emotions. We are still, as I see it, somewhat in disbelief at the scope that
70 technology has assumed in only a few short decades of human history, and we need to bring it all down to a human level. We greet it with human negatives (disgust, annoyance) and human positives (loyalty, affection) without ever asking whether our emotions really add up.

11

The author of Passage 1 cites the Boston Federal Reserve in line 23 in order to

A) disprove an earlier statement.

B) introduce a paradox.

C) refute a popular conception.

D) present a controversial idea.

12

The main purpose of the second paragraph of Passage 1 (lines 8-18) is to

A) address a common misconception.

B) provide a historical synopsis.

C) anticipate a counter-argument.

D) analyze a personal choice.

CONTINUE

13

The author of Passage 1 characterizes technology as a "handmaiden and a temptress" in order to

A) demonstrate its potential both for progress and destruction.
B) argue that as much as technology saves time it also creates needs.
C) emphasize the association of modern communication technology with women's roles.
D) cast doubt on technology's purportedly humanitarian intentions.

14

As used in line 6, "commands" most nearly means

A) requires.
B) dictates.
C) gains.
D) instructs.

15

Passage 1 and Passage 2 differ in that

A) Passage 1 is concerned with technology's effect on leisure while Passage 2 is concerned with technology's effect on thought.
B) Passage 1 unequivocally condemns modern technology while Passage 2 is more ambivalent.
C) Passage 1 argues for a revised conception of technology while Passage 2 is satisfied with the status quo.
D) Passage 1 is deeply critical of technology while Passage 2 is more circumspect.

16

What would the author of Passage 2 most likely consider "it all" in line 37?

A) "texting" (line 46)
B) "ClownDating" (line 49) and "Pictures of Hipsters Taking Pictures of Food" (line 50)
C) "rapidly delivered forms of entertainment" (line 60)
D) "high emotions" (line 68)

17

The author of Passage 1 would most likely attribute the popularity of new technologies to

A) economic prosperity.
B) spiritual decline.
C) great convenience.
D) alluring advertising.

18

Which choice provides the best evidence for the answer to the previous question?

A) Lines 8-11 ("The devices . . . catch on")
B) Lines 19-22 ("Each of . . . you time")
C) Lines 22-26 ("In fact . . . week")
D) Lines 34-36 ("While working . . . turbocharged")

19

The author of Passage 2 offers his students a curriculum that can best be described as

A) unstable.
B) erudite.
C) investigative.
D) biased.

20

Which choice provides the best evidence for the answer to the previous question?

A) Lines 40-42 ("To gauge . . . though")
B) Lines 47-54 ("The students . . . apart")
C) Lines 58-61 ("The students . . . lives")
D) Lines 62-64 ("While I . . . waned")

21

As used in line 68, "high" most nearly means

A) elevated.
B) sophisticated.
C) intense.
D) lofty.

CONTINUE 163

Test 10

Questions 22-31 are based on the following passage and supplementary material.

This reading is an excerpt from the essay "The Grand Unifying (Geological) Theory" by Eliza Morris.

The theory of plate tectonics posits that Earth's landmasses sit atop massive "plates," which shift with the passage of time. The theory was proposed in the early 1960s, as an answer to
Line the problems with the theory of continental drift. Since that
5 time, the plate tectonic theory has become widely accepted in the scientific community. Yet there remain dissenters, scientists who believe they see problems in the idea of plate tectonics. Though passions can run high over plate tectonics, dissent—even unpopular dissent—is part of the scientific process.
10 Plate tectonics has a long and complicated history. In 1915, Alfred Wegener proposed a theory he called "continental drift." His ideas were based on his observation that Earth's continents could fit together neatly, like puzzle pieces—implying that they once fit together border-to-border. Wegener concluded that
15 Earth's continents must have moved into their present positions over millions of years.
    Wegener got it partially right—according to the theory of plate tectonics—when he said that the continents had moved. Yet Wegener, who was meteorologist and not a geologist,
20 couldn't explain their movement. Scientists of the day pointed to one major hole in his theory: the oceanic crust is much too thick for continents to simply push their way through. It wasn't until the 1960s that scientists were able to propose a better hypothesis: that Earth's continents lie on top of vast plates,
25 which are moved along by the spreading of the seafloor and the interaction of the different layers of the Earth.
    Plate tectonics proposes what is generally referred to as the "conveyor belt principle." This states that as the seafloor spreads outward from the center, the material at the edges gets
30 subducted into the Earth's mantle. The total surface area of the planet remains the same: as new material is introduced, older material is recycled. Another crucial component of plate tectonics is its explanation of volcanic and geologic activity. Scientists have noticed that mountains, deep-sea trenches, and
35 volcanoes all tend to form where the massive plates converge.
    This theory, however, is not without its detractors. In 1996, after a symposium in Beijing, a few scientists formed what they called "The New Concepts in Global Tectonics Group." Concerned with what they saw as shortcomings in the theory
40 of plate tectonics, the leaders wrote: " . . . the Plate Tectonic Theory has swept aside much well-based data as though it never existed . . . result[ing] in the suppression or manipulation of data which does not fit the theory. In the course of time the method has become narrow, monotonous and dull . . . As new
45 data has arisen there is a growing skepticism about the theory." Much of the evidence presented in the group's newsletter proposes an alternative hypothesis, which involves a system of "lineaments" which cover the surface of the Earth.
    Most other critics of plate tectonics point out what they
50 perceive as flaws in the theory, rather than proposing new theories to explain Earth's geology. Far from being a form of mere naysaying, this spirit of refutation is a vital part of how sound scientific practice operates. Indeed, the plate tectonics theory has undergone several important revisions
55 since it was first proposed. Yet it's important to separate the working process of the scientific method (which thrives on the discarding of old, faulty data) from ideological dispute. According to the National Center for Higher Education, plate tectonics continues "to generate social controversy over [its]
60 implications for policy or for personally-held religious views," much as the issues of global warming and evolution do. However, even in the face of the theory's shortcomings, and in reference to politically- or religiously-motivated dissent, the Center states that "plate tectonics [is] not scientifically
65 controversial today."

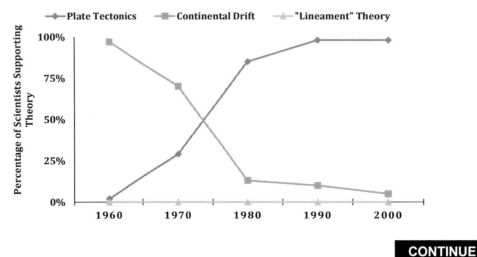

Theory Approval in Scientific Community Regarding Landmass Movement

CONTINUE

22

The passage indicates that the theory of continental drift is

A) not entirely inaccurate, but still incomplete.

B) unhelpful to the scientific process.

C) far-fetched but true.

D) still the best explanation for the movement of landmasses.

23

Which choice provides the best evidence for the answer to the previous question?

A) Lines 3-4 ("The theory . . . drift")

B) Lines 4-6 ("Since that . . . community")

C) Lines 14-16 ("Wegener . . . of years")

D) Lines 17-20 ("Wegener . . . movement")

24

As used in line 24, "vast" most nearly means

A) limitless.

B) profound.

C) immeasurable.

D) tremendous.

25

The main idea of the fourth paragraph (lines 36-48) is that

A) plate tectonic theory does not have very much support.

B) critics of plate tectonic theory argue that its proponents may be manipulating data to confirm their beliefs.

C) the scientific community is experiencing an ideological split that could threaten the objectivity of the scientific method.

D) a new explanation has superseded plate tectonic theory as the most popular landmass theory within the scientific community.

26

The passage suggests that some critics of the theory of plate tectonics may be

A) guilty of skewing data to confirm their own theories.

B) teaming up to attack the reputation of Alfred Wegener.

C) motivated by personal beliefs rather than scientific observations.

D) skeptical of the idea that landmasses are moving.

27

Which choice provides the best evidence for the answer to the previous question?

A) Line 36 ("This theory . . . detractors")

B) Lines 46-48 ("Much of the . . . Earth")

C) Lines 51-53 ("Far from . . . operates")

D) Lines 55-57 ("Yet it's . . . dispute")

28

As used in line 55, "separate" most nearly means

A) quarantine.

B) differentiate.

C) sever.

D) divide.

29

The main purpose of the final paragraph is to

A) distinguish between useful scientific debate and other, less scientific arguments against plate tectonic theory.

B) discuss the relative value of two disparate scientific organizations.

C) advocate for those who take issue with plate tectonics on ideological grounds.

D) criticize scientists who refute plate tectonics without offering a better alternative.

30

Data in the graph indicate that the greatest difference between support for plate tectonic theory and support for continental drift occurred during which year?

A) 1970

B) 1980

C) 1990

D) 2000

31

Data in the graph most strongly support which of the following statements?

A) From 1975 to 2000, plate tectonic theory replaced continental drift as the most popular explanation for the movement of landmasses.

B) Plate tectonic theory has consistently garnered more support than continental drift.

C) The scientific community grew considerably larger between 1980 and 2000.

D) In 2000, the combined support for continental drift and "lineament" theory was greater than support for plate tectonic theory.

Questions 32-41 are based on the following passage.

First introduced in 1923, The Equal Rights Amendment was designed to combat legal and workplace discrimination against women. In this 1970 speech, Congresswoman Shirley Chisholm explains why such an amendment would be a boon to American society.

What would be the economic effects of the Equal Rights Amendment? Direct economic effects would be minor. If any labor laws applying only to women still remained, their
Line amendment or repeal would provide opportunity for women
5 in better-paying jobs in manufacturing. More opportunities in public vocational and graduate schools for women would also tend to open up opportunities in better jobs for women.

The indirect effects could be much greater. The focusing of public attention on the gross legal, economic, and social
10 discrimination against women by hearings and debates in the Federal and State legislatures would result in changes in attitude of parents, educators, and employers that would bring about substantial economic changes in the long run.

Sex prejudice cuts both ways. Men are oppressed by the
15 requirements of the Selective Service Act, by enforced legal guardianship of minors, and by alimony laws. Each sex, I believe, should be liable when necessary to serve and defend this country. Each has a responsibility for the support of children.

There are objections raised to wiping out laws protecting
20 women workers. No one would condone exploitation. But what does sex have to do with it. Working conditions and hours that are harmful to women are harmful to men; wages that are unfair for women are unfair for men. Laws setting employment limitations on the basis of sex are irrational, and the proof of
25 this is their inconsistency from state to state. The physical characteristics of men and women are not fixed, but cover two wide spans that have a great deal of overlap. It is obvious, I think, that a robust woman could be more fit for physical labor than a weak man. The choice of occupation would be determined
30 by individual capabilities, and the rewards for equal works should be equal.

This is what it comes down to: artificial distinctions between persons must be wiped out of the law. Legal discrimination between the sexes is, in almost every instance, founded on
35 outmoded views of society and the pre-scientific beliefs about psychology and physiology. It is time to sweep away these relics of the past and set further generations free of them.

Federal agencies and institutions responsible for the enforcement of equal opportunity laws need the authority of a
40 Constitutional amendment. The 1964 Civil Rights Act and the 1963 Equal Pay Act are not enough; they are limited in their coverage—for instance, one excludes teachers, and the other leaves out administrative and professional women. The Equal Employment Opportunity Commission has not proven to be

CONTINUE

45 an adequate device, with its power limited to investigation, conciliation, and recommendation to the Justice Department. In its cases involving sexual discrimination, it has failed in more than one-half. The Justice Department has been even less effective. It has intervened in only one case involving
50 discrimination on the basis of sex, and this was on a procedural point. In a second case, in which both sexual and racial discrimination were alleged, the racial bias charge was given far greater weight.

Evidence of discrimination on the basis of sex should
55 hardly have to be cited here. It is in the Labor Department's employment and salary figures for anyone who is still in doubt. Its elimination will involve so many changes in our State and Federal laws that, without the authority and impetus of this proposed amendment, it will perhaps take another 194 years.
60 We cannot be parties to continuing a delay. The time is clearly now to put this House on record for the fullest expression of that equality of opportunity which our founding fathers professed. They professed it, but they did not assure it to their daughters, as they tried to do for their sons.
65 The Constitution they wrote was designed to protect the rights of white, male citizens. As there were no black Founding Fathers, there were no founding mothers—a great pity, on both counts. It is not too late to complete the work they left undone. Today, here, we should start to do so.

32

According to Chisholm, the indirect economic effects of the Equal Rights Amendment could be

A) the same as the direct economic effects.

B) less than the direct economic effects.

C) greater than the direct economic effects.

D) impossible to predict.

33

As used in line 14, "cuts" most nearly means

A) exerts a harmful influence.

B) divides people into factions.

C) penetrates.

D) separates.

34

The third paragraph (lines 14-18) serves to

A) show how sexual discrimination affects military personnel.

B) explain why sexual discrimination is mostly aimed at women.

C) argue that there is no difference between men and women.

D) illustrate that discrimination due to sex affects men as well as women.

35

Chisholm's examples of the "robust woman" and "weak man" (lines 28-29) serve to

A) call attention to two forms of sexual discrimination.

B) bring up scenarios that are discussed later on.

C) provide support for the previous sentence.

D) make a broad distinction between men and women.

36

According to the passage, laws that discriminate between the sexes are based on

A) antiquated views in society that predate scientific findings in psychology and physiology.

B) the comparatively primitive psychological research of the time.

C) unfair verdicts made on the basis of sex by the Justice Department.

D) the Constitution as it was originally written by the Founding Fathers.

37

Which choice provides the best evidence for the answer to the previous question?

A) Lines 19-20 ("There . . . workers")

B) Lines 25-27 ("The physical . . . overlap")

C) Lines 33-36 ("Legal . . . psychology")

D) Lines 54-56 ("Evidence . . . doubt")

CONTINUE ➡ 167

38

Chisholm states that existing legislation designed to promote equal opportunity is ultimately

A) fair, as it covers both sexes and all races.

B) inadequate, because it doesn't apply to all vocations.

C) superfluous, because the Constitution applies to everyone.

D) beneficial, as it addresses the exclusions in the Constitution.

39

Which choice provides the best evidence for the answer to the previous question?

A) Lines 23-25 ("Laws . . . State")

B) Lines 32-33 ("This is . . . the law")

C) Lines 40-43 ("The 1964 . . . women")

D) Lines 65-66 ("The Constitution . . . male citizens")

40

In combating sexual discrimination, the Equal Employment Opportunity Commission, in comparison to the Justice Department, is

A) a completely failing organization.

B) more slowly making a positive change.

C) more helpful, but still deficient.

D) more harmful in the long run.

41

As used in line 61, "expression" most nearly means

A) explanation.

B) verbalization.

C) mention.

D) enactment.

Questions 42-52 are based on the following passage and supplementary material.

This passage is adapted from Danielle Barkley, "Major Environmental Problem, Microscopic Solution."

Today, tiny organisms—some so tiny that each one consists of a single cell—are increasingly recognized as assets in solving a variety of scientific problems. One of the most
Line pressing of these problems is the challenge of controlling
5 the methane levels in the Earth's atmosphere. Methane is a chemical compound consisting of one atom of carbon and four atoms of hydrogen; it is produced naturally when larger organic materials are broken down either by microbes or by heat and pressure. Methane is a major component of a major human
10 fuel source, natural gas, and the process of producing, storing, and distributing natural gas results in methane escaping into the atmosphere. Like carbon dioxide, methane is a greenhouse gas: when it enters the atmosphere it absorbs the sun's heat and can contribute to rising temperatures. Estimates suggest that
15 since pre-industrial times, the concentration of methane in the earth's atmosphere has risen 160%. Industry is indeed largely responsible, though other human activities have exacerbated the problem: for example, methane is also produced through the decomposition of the large quantities of organic material in
20 landfill sites.

Among ecologists, environmentalists, and concerned citizens generally, substantial interest in reducing methane emissions has arisen due to methane's potential for environmental disruption. One strategy for achieving methane
25 reduction might be to harness the power of small but mighty microorganisms known as methanotrophs. Like bacteria, methanotrophs are prokaryotes, which means that they are single-celled entities whose cellular structures are not enclosed in separate compartments. In order to survive, methanotrophs
30 metabolize methane: they break down the chemical bonds between atoms and use the resulting carbon as their source of energy. To perform this process, methanotrophs make use of two enzymes, one of which contains copper and the other of which contains iron. Because copper and iron are vital to
35 methanotrophs, these microorganisms cultivate special proteins that allow them to store these chemical elements.

Since methanotrophs rely on methane as their sole source of energy, they can only exist in environments where methane is present in relative abundance. At the same time, they are able
40 to survive extreme temperatures and to tolerate both acidic and alkaline environments. Common habitats for methanotrophs include stretches of soil near marshes, lakes, and agricultural sites. These exceptional microorganisms also exist deep underwater, at sites where methane is released through cracks
45 in the ocean floor. The presence of methanotrophs in these environments is important, since methanotrophs help to regulate and sustain diverse communities of microscopic life

CONTINUE

forms. Thus, when methane occurs naturally, it forms part of a healthy biological system. However, as methane levels become
50 elevated by human activity, the balance is altered.

The existing relationship between methanotrophs and methane makes these organisms a potential tool of great promise for controlling levels of methane emission. There are two main approaches to the study of methanotrophs. One
55 is to learn from what these organisms have evolved to do and to adapt these strategies into ways of making methane less harmful, either before or as it is released. Scientific research related to this approach focuses on obtaining a more detailed picture of how methanotrophs metabolize methane;
60 the hope is that this deepened understanding will generate insight into how humans can likewise render methane more innocuous. A different approach focuses on limiting the quantity of methane that is released. Studies supporting this approach are premised on monitoring the population levels of
65 methanotrophs, ascertaining whether certain environments tend to support higher populations, and encouraging the presence of methanotrophs so as to ensure that the maximum possible amount of methane is consumed rather than released. In either case, the science of methanotrophs suggests that a naturally
70 occurring balance between organisms and their energy source may hold the key to the sustainable use of natural resources on a human level.

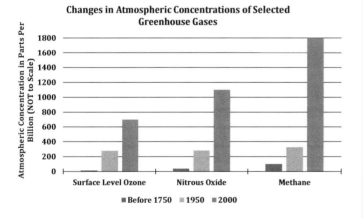

Changes in Atmospheric Concentrations of Selected Greenhouse Gases

42

The author most likely mentions carbon dioxide in the first paragraph to

A) lend authority to the author's claim about the effects of the sun on global temperature.

B) suggest that gases found in the atmosphere typically do not have a warming impact.

C) highlight how unimportant carbon dioxide levels are when compared to methane concentrations.

D) provide a reference point for the reader by introducing a substance comparable to methane.

43

The "ecologists, environmentalists, and concerned citizens" (lines 21-22) would likely describe the recent changes in methane concentration as

A) irreversible.

B) surprising.

C) disturbing.

D) fortuitous.

44

As used in line 32, "perform" most nearly means

A) conduct.

B) show.

C) channel.

D) transmit.

45

The passage indicates that the environments where methanotrophs can thrive are

A) determined by the presence of methane.

B) only in areas where water can be found.

C) not at all overlapping with those of humans.

D) always conducive to methanotrophs' mobility.

46

Which choice provides the best evidence for the answer to the previous question?

A) Lines 26-29 ("Like bacteria . . . compartments")

B) Lines 37-39 ("Since methanotrophs . . . abundance")

C) Lines 43-45 ("These exceptional . . . ocean floor")

D) Lines 63-68 ("Studies supporting . . . than released")

47

As used in line 41, "Common" most nearly means

A) unrefined.

B) widespread.

C) typical.

D) plentiful.

CONTINUE 169

48

The author indicates that people value methanotrophs primarily because they believe that

A) studying methanotrophs will yield knowledge that is useful for mitigating human-sourced emissions.

B) confining methanotrophs to isolated areas will decrease the harm that they inflict on the atmosphere.

C) methanotrophs produce proteins that humans can use in industrial processes.

D) maintaining a healthy methanotroph population worldwide will foster the stability of other microorganism populations.

49

Which choice provides the best evidence for the answer to the previous question?

A) Lines 3-5 ("One of the . . . atmosphere")

B) Lines 34-36 ("Because copper . . . elements")

C) Lines 45-48 ("The presence . . . life forms")

D) Lines 57-62 ("Scientific . . . more innocuous")

50

The graph following the passage offers evidence that the atmosphere has changed since 1750 in that

A) methane is the only greenhouse gas that has become more concentrated.

B) both nitrous oxide and methane have become less concentrated.

C) the concentration of surface level ozone has recently declined.

D) methane, nitrous oxide, and surface level ozone have all become more concentrated.

51

The author would most likely attribute the rise in methane concentration in the atmosphere as represented in the graph to

A) the relative fall in concentrations of other greenhouse gases.

B) the prevalence of industrialization.

C) the decay of organic matter.

D) inadequate use of microorganisms.

52

According to the data in the graph, which of the following choices represents the greatest percentage increase in atmospheric concentration?

A) Surface Level Ozone, 1750-1950

B) Surface Level Ozone, 1950-2000

C) Nitrous Oxide, 1950-2000

D) Methane, 1750-1950

STOP

If you finish before time is called, you may check your work on this section only.
Do not turn to any other section.

No Test Material On This Page

Answer Key: TEST 10

Test 10

PASSAGE 1
Fiction

1. C
2. D
3. D
4. D
5. D
6. A
7. B
8. C
9. C
10. B

PASSAGE 2
Social Science

11. B
12. B
13. B
14. B
15. A
16. C
17. D
18. B
19. C
20. A
21. C

PASSAGE 3
Natural Science 1

22. A
23. D
24. D
25. B
26. C
27. D
28. B
29. A
30. D
31. A

PASSAGE 4
Global Conversation

32. C
33. A
34. D
35. C
36. A
37. C
38. B
39. C
40. C
41. D

PASSAGE 5
Natural Science 2

42. D
43. C
44. A
45. A
46. B
47. C
48. A
49. D
50. D
51. B
52. A

Once you have determined how many questions
you answered correctly, consult the chart on Page 174
to determine your **SAT Reading Test score.**

Please visit **ies2400.com/answers** for answer explanations.

Post-Test Analysis

This post-test analysis is essential if you want to see an improvement on your next test. Possible reasons for errors on the five passages in this test are listed here. Place check marks next to the types of errors that pertain to you, or write your own types of errors in the blank spaces.

TIMING AND ACCURACY

◇ Spent too long reading individual passages
◇ Spent too long answering each question
◇ Spent too long on a few difficult questions
◇ Felt rushed and made silly mistakes or random errors
◇ Unable to work quickly using textual evidence and POE

Other: _____

APPROACHING THE PASSAGES AND QUESTIONS

◇ Unable to effectively grasp a passage's tone or style
◇ Unable to effectively grasp a passage's topic or stance
◇ Did not understand the context of line references
◇ Did not eliminate false answers using strong evidence
◇ Answered questions using first impressions instead of POE
◇ Answered questions without checking or inserting final answer
◇ Eliminated correct answer during POE
◇ Consistent trouble with Word in Context vocabulary
◇ Consistent trouble with Command of Evidence questions
◇ Consistent trouble with passage comparison questions

Other: _____

> **Use this form** to better analyze your performance. If you don't understand why you made errors, there is no way that you can correct them!

FICTION: # CORRECT_____   # WRONG _____   # OMITTED _____

◇ Could not grasp the roles and attitudes of major characters
◇ Could not grasp the significance of particular scenes or images
◇ Difficulty understanding the author's style and language
◇ Difficulty understanding the tone, theme, and structure of the passage as a whole

Other: _____

SOCIAL SCIENCE AND
GLOBAL CONVERSATION: # CORRECT_____   # WRONG _____   # OMITTED _____

◇ Unable to grasp the overall argument or thesis of an individual passage
◇ Unable to work effectively with the specific data or evidence in a passage
◇ Unable to respond effectively to tone, structure, and vocabulary
◇ Difficulty working with the graphics and graphic questions in a Social Science passage
◇ Difficulty understanding the logic or methodology of a Social Science passage
◇ Difficulty with the style and language of a Global Conversation passage
◇ Difficulty with the main historical and political concepts of a Global Conversation passage

Other: _____

NATURAL SCIENCE: # CORRECT_____   # WRONG _____   # OMITTED _____

◇ Unable to grasp the overall argument or thesis of an individual passage
◇ Unable to work effectively with the specific data or evidence in a passage
◇ Unable to respond effectively to tone, structure, and vocabulary
◇ Difficulty understanding the significance of the theories or experiments presented
◇ Difficulty working with the graphics and graphic questions

Other: _____

New SAT Reading: Scoring System

The New SAT combines a converted Reading Score (10-40 scale) with a converted Writing Score (10-40 scale) for a total Scaled Score of 200-800. Simply add the Reading and Writing Scores and multiply by 10. The Reading Score conversion for this book is listed below.

Questions Correct	Reading Score Range	Questions Correct	Reading Score Range	Questions Correct	Reading Score Range
52	40	34	30-29	16	21-20
51	40-39	33	29-28	15	20
50	39-38	32	29-28	14	19
49	38-37	31	29-28	13	19
48	38-37	30	28-27	12	18
47	37-36	29	28-27	11	17
46	37-35	28	27-26	10	17
45	36-35	27	27-25	9	16
44	35-34	26	26-25	8	15
43	35-34	25	25-24	7	15
42	34-33	24	25-24	6	14
41	33-32	23	25-24	5	13
40	33-32	22	24-23	4	12
39	32-31	21	24-23	3	11
38	32-31	20	23-22	2	10
37	31-30	19	22-21	1	10
36	31-30	18	22-21	0	10
35	30-29	17	21-20		

TOTAL SCORE: To obtain your total score out of 800, pair one of the tests in this book with a Writing Test from the IES New SAT Grammar Practice Book or New SAT Verbal Tests. You can learn more about these other titles at ies2400.com.